THORNABY AERODROM
and
WARTIME MEMORIES

by

David Brown

A brief account of life and the goings on at **THORNABY** Aerodrome... the Buildings, Defences, work done and Off Duty moments..... the flying accidents and crashes in **Cleveland**... and the roles played by **GREATHAM** Aerodrome and the importance of **TEESSIDE** industry during **World War Two**.

INTRODUCTION

There are those who thought that Thornaby aerodrome, on the doorstep of industrial Teesside, was a place of fascination and joy.... to others a few metal sheds and huts.... and to others a place of noise where young men risked their lives going up in their fragile flying machines.... and for some, what went on over there remained a complete mystery. In fact fifty years ago Thornaby aerodrome was striving to keep pace with the rapid intake of airmen and aircraft needed to ensure that RAF Thornaby played its' part to the full during World War Two whilst local industry was switched from supplying peacetime needs to meeting wartime requirements.

War was announced on 3 September 1939 at 11.00am and Greatham airfield was requisitioned by RAF Thornaby. The first air raid over Teesside was on 19 May 1940 at West Hartlepool. More urgent defence preparations were made as the Battle of Britain became more imminent as evidenced by Hitler's decree on 16 July 1940. This **brief account**, aims to recreate a picture of 'The life and goings on at **RAF Thornaby** during **World War Two**'.... the forever changing activity... the airfield buildings...the defences necessary to combat the Luftwaffe menace... 'Our Battle of Britain'... the accidents and the kind of `operations work' carried out... the work done by RAF ground personnel... recollections of some 'Off Duty' moments....and the role played by **Greatham airfield**. Mention is also made of other incidents which happened throughout **Cleveland** during wartime, the significant part played by local industry and prewar developments.

Life at Thornaby went on at a yo-yo tempo...up and down. Many men and women who served at Thornaby were often witness to the sacrifice of aircraft and crew which failed to return from war operations or had a flying accident. **Thornaby cemetery** is a unique epitaph to those airmen of all nationalities, both allies and enemy, who were destined not to survive the war. RAF Thornaby was favoured with a spirit of comradeship inherited from the **608** Auxiliary Air Force Squadron going way back to 1930...This spirit helped the people who worked and lived there to tolerate and accept as part of life, the traumas and tribulations of war. Familiar landmarks like the Water Tower and Thornaby Hall have gone ... to quench the needs of the bulldozer when the new Town Centre fringed by Ingleby Barwick and Acklam was developed but traces of the aerodrome can still be seen as mentioned in the following pages.

ABBREVIATIONS

Equivilent Ranks - Royal Air Force (RAF) and German Air Force (Luftwaffe).

G/C	Group Captain (Groupy)	Obst	Oberst
W/C	Wing Commander (Wingco)	Obstltn	Oberstleutnant
S/L	Squadron Leader	Maj	Major
F/L	Flight Lieutenant (Flight Louie)	Hptmn	Hauptmann
F/O	Flying Officer	Oblt	Oberleutnant
P/O	Pilot Officer	Lt	Leutnant
W/O	Warrant Officer	Stfw	Stabsfeldwebel
F/S	Flight Sergeant (Chiefy)	Obfw	Oberfeldwebel
Sgt	Sergeant	Fw	Feldwebel
Cpl	Corporal	Uffz	Unteroffizier
LAC	Leading Aircraftsman	Obgefr	Obergefreiter
AC1	Aircraftsman First Class	Gefr	Gefreiter
AC2	Aircraftsman Second Class	Flgr	Flieger

NCO or other Ranks (Erks)

Common References

WWII	World War Two
CH	Chain Home Radar Station
CHL	Chain Home Low Level Radar
W/T	Wireless Telegraphy
Ack-ack	Anti aircraft guns
HE	Heavy Explosive Bomb
IC	Incendiary Bomb
UXB	Unexploded Bomb
A/T	Anti-tank
Q	Decoy nighttime Airfield
QL	Decoy nighttime Light Site
QF	Decoy nighttime Fire Site
K	Decoy Daytime Airfield (Spoof)
DBR	Damaged beyond repair
U/S	Unserviceable
LMG	Lewis Machine Gun
LAA	Light Anti-aircraft
HAA	Heavy Anti-aircraft
LC	Landing Craft
LCT	Tank Landing Craft
LCS	Tank Landing Ship
KD	Knock Down ship assembly kit

Aircraft

Ar	Arado
Do	Dornier
Fw	Focke Wulf
He	Heinkel
Ju	Junkers
Me	Messerschmitt

Slang

Ammo	Ammunition
Blackouts	WAAF knickers - winter issue
Bumf	Leaflets or Bum-fodder (paper)
Drink	In the, Crash in the Sea
Eggs	Lay, Drop mines in enemy waters
Flip	A short flight in an aircraft
Gen	Information of any kind
Kipper Patrol	Protecting North Sea fishing fleets
Mae West	Inflatable life-saving waist coat, named after the bust of the actress
Pancake	To crash land an aircraft wheels up
Prang	to crash
Queen Bee	Senior Admn. WAAF on a Station
Queen Mary	Long, low slung articulated vehicle
Rookie	A recruit
Scotch Mist	Implies bad eye sight
Shaky Do	Dangerous Operation
Shooting a line	Exaggerated talk
Snowdrop	RAF Policeman
Square-Bashing	Drill on the paradeSquare
Stooge	Stand-in
Tear a strip off	Reprove severely
Tiddly	Intoxicated
Tin Fish	Torpedo
Wizard	First Class
Write-off	Crashed aircraft beyond repair

Personnel

CO	Commanding Officer
SHQ	Station Head Quarters
GR	General Reconnaissance
RAAF	Royal Australian Air Force
RCAF	Royal Canadian Air Force
RNZAF	Royal New Zealand Air Force
USAAF	US Army Air Force
OTU	Operational Training Unit
ATS	Air Training School
FTS	Flying Training School
RN	Royal Navy
Sdn	Squadron
ASR	Air Sea Rescue
BAT	Beam Approach Training
MU	Maintenance Unit
ACS	Airfield Construction Service
ROC	Royal Observer Corp
WAAF	Womens Auxilliary Air Force
AG	Air Gunner
WOp	Wireless Operator
Ob	Observer
GG	Ground Gunner
LDV	Local Defence Volunteer
NDC	National Defence Corps
ATC	Air Training Corps
ARP	Air Raid Wardens (Police)
AFS	Auxilliary Fire Service
NAAFI	Navy, Army & Air Force INSTITUT
ENSA	Enterainments National Service Assn
POW	Prisoner of War

PEACE AND POLITICS

Peacetime flying at Thornaby aerodrome flourished.... although not without intervention from MPs, Town Clerks and even the Air Ministry.

Flying at Thornaby used to take place before the first World War when an early flying pioneer named Hamel hired a field from Matthew Young of The Vale Farm for 100 gold sovereigns for a North of England Air Show. This same field was used during the 1914 to 1918 War by the Royal Flying Corps as a staging post for the aerodromes at Marske and Catterick. During the late 1920's the Air Ministry bought Thornaby Hall from the Crosthwaite family together with some 50 acres of land from Thornaby Grange, The Vale Farm, Thornaby Lodge Farm, Frankland's Farm at Stainsby and Harry Foggin. By early 1930 the road leading to Thornaby Hall was widened and a corrugated iron aeroplane shed, watch hut and various brick buildings were erected (see map). By late 1932 the aerodrome consisted of the Officers Quarters in old Thornaby Hall, four staff cottages, one hanger, Drill room and Mess room covering 194 acres.

The **FIRST** regular Royal Air Force Unit based at Thornaby was the 9 FTS from March 1936 to early 1937. Huts were erected for airmen and 'Bessoneaux' canvas hangers were used for **Hawker Hart Trainers**. During 1937 the Clerk of Works and his staff were constantly under pressure to ensure that the grass landing field, buildings and accommodation were in a usable condition at all times. The increased activity was reflected in the number of incidents. During one week, for instance, nine **Demons** had to be scrapped. During 1938, the nearby airfield at Greatham was selected in favour of Marske for development as Thornaby's satellite airfield. Thornaby Council disapproved of airfield activities from the start. It objected to bombing practice during 1932 and refused to permit the closure of Millbank Lane at weekends. Two years later, complaints from local residents about machine gun fire resulted in a 'noise ban' being imposed during Sunday church going hours. Then during 1936, Mr.Harold McMillan MP was petitioned by locals to seek the removal of the machine gun butts and the engine testing shed away from near Millbank Lane to 'elsewhere'. It was alleged that the noise caused children in prams to scream in terror, horses to bolt, dogs to bark and people asleep to awake in terror. After much hassle, additional land was acquired by the Air Ministry and the butts and the testing shed were moved to the south east part of the airfield. Ironically whilst Hither busily continued to expand the German Luftwaffe (air force) in contravention of the Treaty of Versailles and occupied Rhineland and Austria, the growth of activity at RAF Thornaby continued to be hampered by arguments with the Town Clerk concerning Planning regulations about wooden huts, Drill Hall, roads, the closure of bridle paths and fencing, and the construction of a water tower so as to ensure the provision of appropriate water supplies,

608 (North Riding) Auxiliary Air Force **Bomber** Squadron was formed on **17 March 1930** with one Officer (F/L.C.L.Falconer) and eleven airmen. Flying Instructor **S/L.Howard Davies** was in command of the squadron's **Avro 504N Lynx Trainer** aircraft and **Westland Wapitis**. Officer intake was mainly from local business families who were willing to give up their time freely. The first pilot officer (P/O) from 608 Sdn to be gazetted was G.Shaw of W.Shaw Engineering Co on 28 August 1930, followed by I.W.H.Thomson on 29 August 1930, A.N.Wilson on 10 February 1931 and H.Clayton and the well known textile tycoon G.H.Ambler (later Air Vice Marshal) on 17 March, K.Pyman on 27 March, drapery businessman J.Newhouse on 5 July and C.W.Wright on 19 August 1931. Including flying instructor G.Bearne (ex 501 sdn) and F/O.S.R.Groom, 11 officers and 45 other ranks attended the Annual Camp at Thornaby for 14 days on 9 August 1931 for flying training and sports events and encourage airmen to obtain flying experience, albeit as ballast.

During 1932 **S/L.I.W.Thomson** was appointed CO and in December 1934 **S/L.G.H.Ambler** took over command of **608** auxiliaries. Even at this time it was obvious that the German air force was rapidly rearming at a rate of about 300 planes each month. By 1937 Germany had almost twice as many aircraft as Britain. But politics, policies and peace considerations, contrived to ensure that not until late 1937 were plans in hand to allow the British aircraft industry to produce 12,000 planes by early 1940. In 1937 priority was given to bomber production then a year later fewer bombers and more fighters. After the Munich crisis by late 1938, the emphasis was on creating modern fighter aircraft. Each change of policy affected the role played by RAF Thornaby. During 1937 the **608** sdn was designated a **Bomber** squadron of No.6 Auxiliary Group equipped with **Westland Wallace** bombers. Then on 14 January 1937 the squadron started to convert to **Demon** fighters which remained at Thornaby until 20 March 1939 when they were replaced by **Anson** (GR) aircraft. On 5 May 1937 **608** sdn became the North Riding **Fighter** Sdn on joining No.12 (Fighter) Group **and remained** so until 20 March 1939, when it became a **GR** squadron to counter the potential German menace to shipping off the North East coast. S/L.G.Shaw replaced S/L.Ambler as CO **608** sdn during October 1938.

The **FIRST** Station HQ was established at RAF Thornaby as part of No.16 Reconnaissance Group of Coastal Command on **1 June 1937**, commanded initially by W/C.J.Leacroft until G/C.A.H.Jackson took over on 15 November followed by W/C.L.G.le.B.Croke on 24 January 1938, G/C.Grenfell on 12 May and W/C.S.P.Simpson (later G/C) on 4 August 1938. A different role was effected as part of No.5 Bomber Command from 1 September 1938 until 20 March 1939 when the Station joined No.18 (Reconnaissance) Group of Coastal Command apart from a brief spell with No.16 (Reconnaissance) Coastal Command whilst awaiting the outcome of Munich Talks from 28 September until 10 October 1938.

The tempo changed at RAF Thornaby to a less peaceful, more purposeful mood as the '**Auxiliaries**' were joined by two General Reconnaissance (GR) squadrons, **233** sdn on 18 May 1937 and then **224** sdn on 9 July 1937. These two squadrons' 48 **Ansons** supported by **608** Sdns' **Demons**, **Hart Tutors** and **Avro trainers** provided a substantial force of more than 60 aircraft. By September 1938, **224** sdn had moved to Leuchars on 29 August followed by **233** sdn three days later. **Fairey Battles** of **106** (Newcastle Own) and **185** (West Hartlepool Own) sdns arrived on 1 September 1938 and stayed continuously at Thornaby, except at the time of the 'Munich' War Alert during which time both squadrons reequipped with **Hampdens** before moving to Cottesmore during August 1939.

They were then replaced by **Ansons** of **220** sdn. At the time of the Munich crisis Ansons of **269** (GR) sdn and Wildebeests of **42** (Torpedo bomber) sdn. replaced 106 and 185 sdns at Thornaby for a few days until 10 October 1938 and detachments of Royal Artillery ack-ack and Green Howards were alerted for local defence duties

As 'Munich' passed by so did the sixth and last impressive Empire Day flying Displays take place on 20 May 1939. Appeals were made for recruits to the Civil Air guard and RAFVR at Greatham and Thornaby. As the likelihood of war loomed closer, so during mid 1939 were the squadrons and HQ at RAF Thornaby flooded with Air Ministry regulations. One related to 'The WAAFs' which was formed on 28 June 1939 so allowing women to join the Royal Air Force and another permitted civilians to be employed by the RAF. Another dealt with the age of aircrew (18 years) needed to fly Britains 4,000 air planes

Conscription started during May 1939 and young men aged 20 and 21 years started to enlist. Later the National Services Act (Armed Forces) made those men aged from 18 to 41 years of age liable to conscription starting on 21 October 1939. Men aged 41 years were conscripted in June 1941. Deferment from call up was allowed for those employed in reserved occupations coal mining or steel making industries or having a key skill essential for making weapons or growing food, or constructing ships, hangers and aircraft.

When war started the assortment of 8,000 air planes in service by the combined British and French Air Forces was numerically equal to the Luftwaffe but as events soon proved were less effective. The RAF had just 500 or one third as many first line bombers as the Luftwaffe and about 600 first line fighters equal to about half similar German aircraft. The enemy also had over 800 reconnaissance airplanes, which was twice as many as the combined British Fleet Air Arm, Reconnaissance and Coastal Commands could muster. Coastal Command had 19 squadrons equipped with a mixture of flying boats and short range Wildebeests, Hudsons and Ansons, a force of 252 aircraft of which an initial establishment 36 **Ansons** plus reserves were based at RAF Thornaby used by **220** and **608** squadrons. All that was needed was the men to keep them flying.

Hawker Demon K3779 at 608 sdn Summer Camp, WARMWELL. Commanding Officer S/L. G. H. Ambler (1st Left). 1938

Avro Anson L of 220 sdn flying over HMS Furious prewar

Westland Wapiti Bomber K7310 hit an ambulance on take off from Thornaby & was wrecked. May 1937

One of the FIRST Hawker Hurricanes at Thornaby Aerodrome being refuelled by `Tug`Wilson & Steve Martin on 20 June 1938.

HM King George VI visits Thornaby Aerodrome. HM is accompanied by Sir Cyril Newall (Chief of Air Staff) & Sir Fred Bowhill (AOC Coastal Command).   November 1939.

Avro Anson of 224 sdn on patrol over a Wartime Convoy.

FOREVER CHANGING

One of the few things that remained unchanged at RAF Thornaby during World War Two was the address **Royal Air Force Station, No.18 Group, Coastal Command, Thornaby Road, Thornaby-on-Tees.** Changes occured at an amazing pace as different squadrons, aircraft and people continually came and went so as to meet the ever changing needs of war.

On 12 August 1939, the 608 North Riding GR squadron and families were transported to Thornaby station and then continued by 'Special' train to attend their annual camp at Warmwell, near Weymouth in Dorset. Whilst there, they took part in combined exercises at No.6 ATS at Blandford in Dorset involving Royal Navy (RN) submarines and visited HM Dockyards at Portsmouth. On 23 August 1939 a signal was received which instructed the squadron of 24 Officers and 278 other ranks together with 18 Ansons, one Hart and two Tutors aircraft to prepare to return to Thornaby. The airfield at Thornaby became rapidly congested and obstructed by returning aircraft. Due to bad weather some aircraft failed to make home base and landed elsewhere. Airman and officers with full kit, eventually arrived by train at Stockton station at noon on 28 August and were led by the RAF Band in a march along Stockton High Street en route to RAF Thornaby... in contrast to the stylish outward journey. Airmen of married status accompanied their families via train to Thornaby station. On arrival at RAF Thornaby many lower ranks were deployed on jankers like tasks essential to feed and accommodate the hoards of recruits and or shifting bombs. Others were sent for training somewhere in the UK.

By 24 August 1939 the North Riding **608** sdn was embodied into the RAF for full time duties. Meanwhile, call up notices were being issued to Reservists and by 1 September the squadrons were fully mobilised for war with Germany and appropriate precautions were hastily put into operation. Vetos were imposed on W/T and hand books were not to be carried in aircraft. On 3 September 1939 all officers and men were initially confined to camp. This order was later rescinded due to complaints by married men who were used to living out and lack of accommodation. Houses in the vicinity of Bassleton Road were requisitioned for RAF and military purposes. Most men were billeted in hangers or bell tents, each capable of accommodating 12 men.

Airplanes had nothing but the basic or maybe less than basic essentials fitted. One airman praised **Hudsons** as compared with Ansons for having all sorts of things including a bed and lavatory! Two days after war was declared **220** sdn started converting from **Ansons** to Lockheed **Hudson mk1s**, a task which was completed by December 1939. A detachment of Hudsons **224** squadron from Leuchars which stayed at Thornaby whilst **220** squadron learned to fly Hudsons, suffered the loss of at least 22 crew whilst doing the work of **220** sdn.

The **FIRST** fatality at Thornaby was P/O.J.Scott who was killed in a motor cycle accident at the New Inn, Maltby when his machine missed the turning in the road. He was buried with full military honours on 9 October 1939 at West Hartlepool.

During October 1939 men started to be billeted in the Drill Hall and huts. By early November men in the Drill hall had been moved to huts thereby enabling that most essential establishment the NAAFI to resume normal duties.

Concern was voiced about Ack-ack gunners shooting at friendly aircraft. During the period January 1940 until July 1941 detachments of three **Spitfires** from **41** sdn along with officers and men, alternated with **54** sdn at Thornabys' front line satellite airfield at **Greatham**. The home based **608** sdn whose total strength in January 1940 was 17 officers (11 pilots, two air gunners, four ground duties) and 347 men was reorganised into three flights. Together with ground support and other squadrons, in excess of 2,000 airmen, airwomen and civilians were based at RAF Thornaby. Apart from the Ansons of **608** sdn and the Hudsons of **220** sdn, Hurricanes from the local **607** City of Durham fighter squadron from RAF **Usworth** also called during this period and several unfamiliar aircraft had to make emergency calls at Thornaby.

King George V1's visit to RAF Thornaby on 1 November 1939 was not witnessed by many although most were aware of the presence of a VIP visitor. His Majesty accompanied by Queen Elizabeth and Sir Frederick Bowhill (Commander of Air Staff), Air Commander Breeze and G/C Simpson inspected a guard of Green Howards and visited the

Radar station at **Danby**...... and so one story goes were refused entry by the Green Howards on duty until G/C Simpson could produce his 1250 identification card. Due to this incident and the avid interest shown by their Majesties lunch had to be postponed until 3.00pm on their return to RAF Thornaby.

Weather, especially bad weather played havoc with station preparedness. Aircraft were apt to bog down and Ansons were suffering from exposure. The state of the airfield was attributed as the cause for several **220** sdn Ansons suffering collapsed under carriages necessitating major repair work. Due to the arctic like conditions prevailing during December it was decided, regardless of security regulations and interference with servicing schedules, to keep three aircraft in each hanger as a safeguard against the cold. Later in January 1940 snow and frost affected all activities in some way and runways were not serviceable until heavy rolling equipment was called up for action. Snowfalls of up to twelve inches per day were not uncommon and snow drifts up to nose height of some aircraft, prevented aircraft from to taking off. When the thaw came runways surfaces were too slushy or entirely under water to enable Ansons to operate safely. Fire pumps when used in attempts to clear the runways found that icing problems at best left only the shortest runway usable.

By April 1940 the station had become wholly congested. A solution was partially found by **608** sdn being confined to the north side and **220** sdn being located on the south side of the airfield. A detachment from **224** sdn was again based at Thornaby during June during the evacuation of Dunkirk.

After a visit by Lord Trenchard during June **608** sdn was instructed to re equip with Blackburn **Bothas** which were totally under powered, using nine cylinder engines instead of the originally intended fourteen cylinder Bristol Pegasus engines which were needed for Blenheim, Beauforts and Beaufighters. On 28 June the first of the 'dreaded' **Bothas** arrived. During the transition stage a mixture of **Bothas** and **Ansons** were flown by **608** sdn. But eventually **Bothas**, due to handling problems caused by the engines developing cracks around the cabin and cat-walks and the inability to take off with a torpedo bomb load, necessitated the reissue on 26 August of faithful 'Annie' **Anson**. On 17 September **Bothas** were abandoned and were sent to MUs for further investigation. To cover for the short comings of the **Botha**, Swordfish aircraft of Royal Navy **812** sdn from North Coates were occasionally on duty at Thornaby from 27 September 1940 onwards.

One year after hostilities the old squadrons' esprit de corps was becoming more difficult to retain, since the character of the prewar 'Auxiliary' and 'Voluntary Reserve' squadrons was gradually being affected by replacement intakes from other squadrons. The aircrew car park gradually filled with vehicles left by men who were fated never to return..... One story recalled how one pilot returned to Thornaby to claim his car only to find that it had been auctioned off.

An unofficial truce was allegedly observed for Xmas 1940, between Britain and Germany from Xmas Eve until Boxing Day, although weather conditions were so bad in Britain and on the Continent, that bomber missions would have been most unlikely in any event.

Following heavy losses in the Battle of the Atlantic in early 1941, Coastal Command was strengthened by **Blenheim** fighter bombers. During April 1941 Coastal Command came under the control of the Royal Navy and some pilots from the **Fleet Air Arm** joined **608** sdn. By this time **608** sdn carried out more offensive missions off Norwegian and Danish coasts, having converted to **Blenheim mkIVs** in February 1941. Subsequently **608** sdn reequipped with **Hudsons** some of which were fitted with air borne radar during July 1941. **W/C.G.Shaw** left Thornaby during May 1941 and was replaced as CO of **608** sdn by **W/C.R.S.Darbyshire** who was followed by **W/C.P.D.R.Hutchings** on 5 November 1941 prior to the squadron moving to Wick in Scotland in January 1942. Meanwhile the **Hudsons** of **220** sdn left Thornaby in April 1941 for Wick and were replaced on 2 March by **Blenheim mkIVs** of **114** (Hong Kong) sdn which took part in escort duties, anti shipping and submarine patrols until being posted to Leuchars in Scotland on 13 May 1941.

The **Air Training Corps** was formed on 5 February 1941, commanded by S/L David Wheldon, to provide 'initial training' for aspiring young airmen.

OTUs commanded first by **S/L.Craven** and then by **W/C.C.D.Candy** (later Air vice Marshal - RAAF) arrived.

6(C)OTU formed from half No.2 School of Army Cooperation based at Andover, was the first unit to arrive, on 19 July 1941 to train Anson and Hudson crews. Immediately on arrival the NCOs and airmen were lined up and randomly divided into A,B and C flights as were the 25 **Hudsons** and instructors, 'A' Flight commander was **S/L.Leach** ex 224 sdn, 'B' Flight was S/L.Spotswood ex 209 sdn (later Marshal of the RAF) and 'C' Flight was **F/L.Jim Peterson** i/c **Ansons** and **Lysanders**. Alongside trainee air crew, were technicians from 83 MU who were being trained by civilian contractors Cuncliffe Owen Aircraft in the art of repairing Hudsons. During March 1943 6(C)OTU changed places with **1(C)OTU** from Silloth for further training of Hudson crews. 1(C)OTU remained at Thornaby until disbandment in October 1943. The OTUs rekindled the great spirit of **608** and **220** sdns attributed to many of the instructors being ex operations from **220/608** sdns. To those returning at a later date after the OTUs had moved on, it seemed that for a while Thornaby had lost its' esprit de corps. During this period RAF Thornaby was commanded by **W/C.C.D.Candy** from 10 December 1941 followed by **G/C.E.D.H.Davies** in February 1942, **G/C.M.H. Kelly** as Chief Flying Instructor on 13 July 1942 and **G/C.B.Paddon** on 28 August 1943.

In March 1941 the recently formed **143** sdn from Coastal Command strike force at Aldergrove, arrived with **Beaufighter mk1cs** until October 1941. **BAT 1509** Flight by this time had formed at Thornaby and stayed until 6 April 1942 before moving on to Church Lawford. From 17 April 1942 until 1 December 1943 N Flight of No.1 Anti aircraft cooperation unit (later **1613** flight) flew **Tiger Moths** and **Henleys** from Thornaby some of which were transferred to Greatham on 4 May 1942.

Spitfires mkVbs of **332** (Norway) sdn were detached from Catterick to **Greatham** on 16 January 1942, then were replaced by four **Spitfire mkVbs** on 19 June 1942 of **403** RCAF sdn. Another four **Spitfire mkVbs** detachment of **401** RCAF sdn arrived at **Thornaby** on 22 January 1943, and changed places with **Spitfire mkVbs** of **306** Polish sdn on 30 May 1943. The Polish squadron stayed until 11 August 1943. The Spitfires were used on convoy patrol duties and remained on call at Greatham whilst shipping convoys passed through this area thereby easing continuous patrol work by **Ansons** and **Hudsons**, as well as providing airfield defensive cover and protection for OTUs.

The skies around Teesside were filled with aircraft of different types. Towards the end of 1942 it was quite normal to see **Ansons** and **Hudsons**, **Lysanders**, **Oxfords**, **Beaufighters**, **Whitleys** and **Wellingtons** and **Spitfires**. **Halifaxes** were seen from Middleton St.George. **Mustangs** from Army Co-operation units and **Hurricanes** were seen as were more and more **Lancasters** and some Coastal Command **Fortresses** and USAAF **Liberators** and many other aircraft. Large formations of **Spitfire** squadrons often over flew the area whilst changing stations as did aircraft with yellow painted under sides which signified aircrew under training.

At nearby Middleton St.George airfield, by the end of 1942, **HalifaxIIs** of the RCAF **Moose** sdn and **WellingtonIIIs** of the **Snowy Owl** sdn had arrived accompanied by **WellingtonIIIs** of the **Lion** sdn at Croft. **Halifaxes** and **Wellingtons** were operational over enemy targets on most nights from Croft and Middleton St.George. Typically 13 **Wellingtons** and 13 **Halifaxes** participated in raids on 10 April 1943, 30 **Halifaxes** took part in raids on Hamburg on 27 July 1943, a similar number were involved in Peenemunde raids on 17 August 1943 and 31 in Berlin raids on 23 August 1943. Losses both of Canadian aircrew and aircraft were extremely high during these raids.

The formation of the 2nd TAF during June 1943 brought various detachments due to troop exercises and troop movements. **Wellingtons** started to disappear from local bomber squadrons and were replaced by USAAF planes.

On 20 October 1943 an **ASR training unit** using mainly **Warwick** aircraft arrived at Thornaby for a few weeks and returned on 21 November and again during March 1944 until May 1944. The **FIRST** ASR sdn to join Thornaby was **280** sdn which started to convert from **Ansons** to **Warwicks** on 21 October 1943. The ASR crew invented the Thornaby bag which was a container of food and first aid which could be dropped to ditched aircrew. **WarwickIs** with cruising speed of 210 mph and armed with eight .303 machine guns were inevitably noticed carrying what was in fact a 23ft 6inch long wooden twin engined and sail lifeboat. It was attached to the bomb bay and could be dropped by parachute to save airmen adrift at sea. On 22 November 1943 came ASR **281** sdn to join **280** sdn, until being posted to Tiree in February 1944. A detachment from **280** sdn were sent to Thorney Island in December 1943 before moving to Strubby in April/May 1944. An operational detachment of **Warwicks** were left at Thornaby and were there at D Day and stayed until **280** sdn returned from from war time operations. The ASR **Warwicks** were often accompanied by **Defiants, Walruses, Sea Otters, Lysanders** and **Martinets** during the training of coastal command crews.

After the OTUs had gone, Coastal Command **Fortresses** and **Halifaxes** sometimes visited Thornaby. It was regular practice, due to bad weather conditions elsewhere or in emergencies to divert bombers returning from operations to Thornaby or Middleton St.George, as for instance the unscheduled arrival of **Lancasters** from **460** squadron at 7.00am at M.St.G on 3 January 1944. **Horsa Gliders** could be seen being towed by **Halifaxes, Whitleys, Dakotas** and **Abermerles. Hurricanes, Lysanders** and **Martinets** were often used for target towing. USAAF planes such as **Liberators** and **Fortresses** were often seen alongside **Marauder** fighters flying very low. Occasionally U.S Troop carriers arrived and offered goodwill lifts in their Liberators. Come February 1944 looking sky-wards unusual formations of combined RAF and USAAF were often noticeable. Leading up to D Day Hadrian gliders were towed by **Abermerle** aircraft from Thornaby, one glider laying claim to having been towed across the Atlantic! At Middleton St.George RCAF **419** sdn. re-equipped with **LancasterXs** during March 1944. During April **Liberators** and **Fortresses** were often seen. Then, leading up to D Day, as bombing operations switched to France, **Halifaxes** and **Lancasters** from **419** Moose sdn and other No.6 RCAF Group airfields in this area were very evident. **Fortresses**, with the familiar painted ladies on their fuselages, most probably used as troop carriers, were also observed on the airfield.

A Vickers Warwick of 279 ASR sdn and lifeboat which is normally seen hanging from the underside of the plane.

After D Day, there was not much flying activity until a third ASR sdn, No.279, arrived on 31 October 1944 from Bircham Newton converting to **Warwicks** from old **Hudsons**. Supported later by **Hurricanes** during Spring 1945 the sdn remained at Thornaby for the duration of the war until 3 September 1945 when it left for Beccles to fly **Lancasters**. G/C.Hon.E.Ward (later standing as parliamentary candidate for Stockton) became CO RAF Thornaby on 18 October 1944 until 7 October 1945. It was after D Day that the first V flying bomb crossed the British coast at Gravesend on 13 June 1944 and the first V2 landed at Chiswick, London on 7 September 1944. A flying bomb buzzed over Billingham and landed about ten miles from Thornaby airfield at Tudhoe on 23 December 1944.

On 3 May 1945 Beaufighters of RAAF **455** sdn arrived from Dallachy to carry out the final offensive action of the war from Thornaby before leaving on the day before VE Day.

By this time Thornaby's own North Riding **608** sdn had been disbanded whilst in Pomigliano, Italy and immediately reformed on **1 August 1944** at Downham Market to fly mosquito bombers until disbandment on 28 August 1945.

VE Day signalled for the disbandment of many squadrons.

HANGERS AND HUTS

Hangers and huts mushroomed around the airfield to cope with the ever increasing numbers of airmen and airwomen. Even at December 1944 nearly two thousand servicemen plus civilian workers.... 130 Officers together with 350 SNCOs and 1153 other ranks and 359 WAAFs were based at Thornaby. Map Reference 93/NZ455163, west of Middlesbrough and adjacent to A1045 was the official location of the airfield. It was sited to the east of Thornaby Village with Stainsby Beck forming the east boundary, Stainsby wood in the south east corner and Thornaby Wood in the south west. By the time of the 'Munich' crisis, during 1938, the technical and servicing area and most other buildings were grouped together in an area north west of the landing fields. Two massive, elegant **'C' type hangers** with their zig-zag roofs, built c.1935, each approximately 235 feet wide by 190 feet long (Ref.33 and 89) of sufficient size to accommodate bomber aircraft, had been installed at either side of the corrugated iron roofed **aeroplane shed** (built in 1929 (Ref.42) and about half as long as the 'C' type), and a **smaller shed** made of similar materials (built in 1931 (Ref.90)). These four hangers formed an arc adjacent to the main cluster of buildings. **Thornaby Hall** and coach house which fronted on to Thornaby Road to the south of the hangers, was used as the officers mess which was considered to be one the best in Britain and nicknamed by some 'The Regent Palace' (like the London Hotel) and reputed as having an excellent chef.

The overall responsibility for airfield buildings and runways rested with the Air Ministry clerk of works, better known as the Works and Bricks Dept. With war being imminent, as the necessary security measures were taken, so were many long overdue improvements and upgradings of the aerodrome put into effect. Blast walls were built to protect petrol tankers and huts, and bulk petrol stores were covered with soil. Rectangular shaped brick wall defence posts each containing two Lewis guns were scattered about. Blocks 1,2,3,4 were sited on the grass area between the main hangers and another block was near the NAAFI. The water tower had a well sandbagged walled surround with a Lewis gun behind it. Access to the 70 feet high tower was by a vertical steel rung ladder.

It was not until the day previous to war was, that George Wimpey had completed the construction of concrete runways, which typically illustrated a reluctance by H.M.Government to spend money, even though plans were in hand to do so in an emergency! Trench shelters made from timber props were camouflaged with earth to form mounds, and dozens of surface shelters were constructed and scattered around the airfield, some of which were connected by under ground corridors. Roadways were camouflaged with peat.

By November 1939 dispersal points for aircraft and perimeter tracks were completed. Hanger floors for Bellman hangers were concreted by Moorhouse and Barker close to the west side perimeter track and four **Bellmans** had been constructed and erected by Head Wrightsons' by this time. The 'Bellman' hanger (Ref.190), was an austerity version of the 'C' type hanger, (so named after N.S.Bellman ex.Air Ministry), and was 175ft long with 87ft.9" door clearance, sufficient to meet the needs of Thornaby as a Coastal command station. An **'A1' type hanger** (Ref.183) was also erected just south of the 'C' types. The hangerage had to cope with the major servicing needs of 50 to 60 aircraft.

Bomb Disposal Dumps were set up, (where Allensway is today), near stables at the south most area of the airfield near Stainsby Woods as far away as possible from the main buildings on land sloping downwards, and were only partly visible above the ground with adequate loading access for trucks. There were six separate units, each measuring 25 feet square, built of reinforced concrete, and capable of storing 22,000lbs of bombs. A further four units each capable of storing 10,000lbs bombs were built one mile to the south. Camouflage wire netting, supported by strong wires was placed over the top surface so as to avoid detection from enemy reconnaissance air planes. To supplement the **fuel tanks** already being used to the north of the 'C' type hangers, another fuel tank protected by 12 inch thick reinforced concrete was installed in the distant south eastern corner, one problem during construction being how to keep the installation dry by using only a three inch hand pump to eject unwanted water.

Vast numbers of **barrack blocks,** each with their pot bellied iron stove, were erected at Thornaby to cater for the ever increasing numbers of auxiliaries, conscripts, GGs and WAAFs. The prospect of long hours and high pay attracted Irish labour to the area. It being said that their efficiency was determined by the ifluence of the local priest! A regular criticism being that the men who build the aerodromes earn more than the men who fly from them!

Camouflage was the responsibility of the Ministry of Defence. Pre war, attempts were made to paint houses on grass areas and hedges on runways and colour roofs red. Buildings were covered with tar and wood chippings then green and khaki paint was applied as per a camouflage map, using both hand and petrol driven pumps. Runway camouflage created problems even though surfaces were quite satisfactory. The paint used by a Tyneside specialist firm was of no use. Precamouflaged wire mesh was used to disguise awkwardly shaped objects and areas. Livestock was also camouflaged, it being recollected by some, that camp adjutant S/L. 'Dolly' Gray, who was responsible for camp food supplies, insisted on the pigs being camouflaged at the RAF piggery! Windows were blacked out in huts by using gas blankets which doubled as protection against gas attack and light eliminator. In the hangers heavy duty cord was used to control the black curtains suspended from heavy duty rails. All buildings had light tight inner and outer doors and even the light bulbs were partly blacked..... the whole camp was very much blacked out.

Obstacles considered to be a hazard to aircraft along the flight paths were removed...... poplars in Thornaby cemetery were lopped. To combat the heavy snow and floods and to give some protection against the arctic like conditions prevailing midway through the first winter of the war, **Canvas hangers** were used to cover the Hudson aircraft of 220 sdn, in an effort to ensure the continued serviceability of at least some aircraft. At times the entire airfield was unusable.

By early 1940 a brick **'Operations' block** had been built. The brick **watch office**, sited between the two 'C' types and the NW/SE runway, was surrounded by a cavity wall made of corrugated sheets filled with gravel to provide a blast shield and on the opposite side of the airfield a small **hut** was built for use as a base for **patrols** around the eastern stretch of the perimeter. As time rolled by buildings were hastily adapted and modified to meet the ever changing needs. The **link trainer building** became the **Gunnery room** and the wooden buildings near the old timber 'Operations' room were hastily converted by contractors for use as **WAAFs barrack rooms** whilst WAAFs remained asleep therein after night duty. By the end of 1940 and the Battle of Britain won, although it was conceded that Thornaby was not in the best of locations, the weather was usually good so it was decided to upgrade the six inch thick concrete **hardstandings** and **three runways**. The NE/SW runway No.2 was extended at the Acklam end to 3750 feet, the W/E runway No.3 to 2400 feet sloping downwards at the Stainsby Beck end and the NW/SE runway No.1 to 3330 feet. Electric runway lights were installed and dispersal area communication lines around airfield were sunk below ground level using whatever hand tools were available. The camouflaging of roads and buildings and runways was completed by October 1940 and before Christmas 1940 a Blind approach landing system was in use and the **'Dummy' landing airfield** ('spoof') at Grangetown was operational.

Although not as disruptive as the weather, the enemy did cause damage to the airfield on 6 June 1940, though damage was restricted to part of the runway parallel to the hangers and the grassed area alongside. During the winter of 1940/41, efforts made to clear the hangers of excessive snow, by using fire hoses caused snow and water to turn to ice causing the subsequent collapse of at least one Bellman hanger. Later, similar hangers collapsed or had to be demolished.

Rumour had it during 1940 that a ghost dressed in flying gear was to be seen wandering around the hangers that were used for 'servicing'. As likely as not such apparitions were due to lack of sleep and excessive work. Aircraft were placed at various disposal points sited mostly to the east and south of the airfield in readiness for routine daily check and operations. The three flights A, B and C, of 608 sdn were at the north end nearest to the amenities. The latter flight was sited near the present day Blue Lion Hotel at the end of Cunningham Drive near woods 220 sdn was located towards the south end of the airfield.

After the departure of the 'Bothas', steel **Blister hangers** each 90 feet wide (derived from a 'Lamella' design of German origin) with one end closed off, capable of storing one aircraft, were manufactured and installed by Dorman Long and covered with earth as camouflage and protection against incendiary attack. Several of these blister hangers were scattered around the airfield (Ref.322,255,193) along-side the west, north and south peri-tracks.

The first **Roman Catholic chapel** was completed on 25 March 1942. The CO laid the foundation stone two months previous. The venture required £400 for furnishings, much hard work, and one hut which was duly requested by S/L.Pollock, the Roman Catholic chaplain. Miraculously a hut was erected within a week, by sympathetic Irish contractors working on site and so gradually the chapel took shape. Questions were not asked as to where money came from, although it is certain that the occasional 'Cert', tipped by a well known jockey stationed at Thornaby and ridden on Stockton Race Course, was often the source of generous contributions. On St.Patrick's Day, 17 March 1942, Fr.Purcell remembers the first ever all ranks dance being held in a 'big hall' at RAF Thornaby in aid of the new R.C Chapel. Monsignor G/C.Beauchamp, principal chaplain to the RAF ceremoniously opened the chapel on 25 March 1942. The small chapel and harmonium is well remembered by Fr.O'Doherty .

During early 1941 an **Officers Mess** was sited away from Thornaby Hall which was adapted for use as the **Sick Quarters**. Near Thornaby Road not far from the main gate **army** companies occupied **huts** until early 1942 when the huts were taken over by the GGs as part of the RAF Regiment. **Tents** still supplemented huts for accommodation, as late as 1942 until 608 sdn moved to Wick. During 1943 unit 5007 ACS was used for various construction repair jobs at Thornaby. During D Day preparations more **huts** were erected in **Richardsons' field** for use by army personnel. At the Ingleby Barwick end in 1943, **runways** were extended to Class A Standard, designed to take the heaviest bombers at the time. More than 100,000 tons of road making materials were used to lay 30 or 40,000 sq.yards of runways, taxi-ways, and hardstandings and 50 miles of pipes and conduits were installed on and around the airfield. The NE/SW runway No.2 had an effective length of 1968 yards, NW/SE runway No.1 1402 yards and the W/E runway No.3 1397 yards, each runway being 50 yards wide with a 75 yards emergency strip at either side and 100 yards overshoot at either end, and a 50 feet wide peri-track around the edge of the airfield. The extended parts remained uncamouflaged.

The FIRST **ATC** premises were behind Pumphries sugar factory, which were later damaged during air raids and later moved to a Nissen hut at Brewery Bank. On 10 September 1944 at 2.30pm Air Commodore the Earl of Harewood opened the ATC HQ near the Officers Mess on Thornaby aerodrome.

By the cessation of hostilities the airfield at Thornaby was well established with 40 or 50 temporary **Barrack blocks** crammed into the north west corner of the airfield and a further 20 or so used by 'Defence Units' were scattered around the perimeters, all of which at one time or another had been used by WAAFs, airmen, soldiers and officers. A variety of abandoned airfields dot Britains landscapes, some are derelict, some like Thornaby are virtually obliterated. Thornaby airfield closed down in 1958. Today brick buildings still remain but familiar landmarks like the 70 feet high water tower and W/T masts, Thornaby Hall, the watch office and the clusters of timber buildings have given way to quench the needs of the bulldozer when the new Thornaby Town Centre was built.

The main conurbation was located on a roughly triangular piece of land at the north west corner of the airfield bounded by Millbank Lane to the north and Thornaby Road to the west. Many of the original buildings can still be seen. Follow the first side of the triangle along the main thoroughfare, (now called Martinet Road) which runs parallel to Millbank Lane, On the left, next to the site of the **guard house** is the **Sergeants mess** and **NAAFI** built in 1931 (now a Snooker Centre which lays claim to mysterious rattlings of snooker balls caused by a ghostly presence... possibly the same 1940 airman dressed in flying gear who is reputed to haunt the 'British Gas' premises which front on to Millbank Lane). Then the **operations block** together with **airmen's barrack block** built in 1931 (now used by Air Training Corps 1261 sdn and Cleveland Army Cadets), **the water tower** and **AMWD** building (now Cleveland Constabulary) were sited along Millbank Lane. Opposite these buildings (on the other side of Martinet Road) were the **SHQ** (now called 'Randol' house), **MT sheds** (now used by Hargreaves Highways), next to which in Master Road is the armoury built in 1931 still complete with window security bars (now used by Douglas Cameron Motor Services) and the **photographic section**. The second side of the triangle begins when turning into Master Road which was mostly used as the hangerage area. Opposite the armoury are the **main stores** and **workshops** (now used by Appleyards garage) which back on to the 1929 hanger (now used by W & J Riding haulage contractor) and a **small aeroplane** shed behind which is the **parachute store** (both now used by Tristar Vehicle Hire) and the cedar wood **'Technical Stores'** hut (supposed life of ten years) which is still in use as a depot for Smalls' buses. To the south of this shed across the road is the site of the **'C' type** (known as **Hintons** which was destroyed by fire). Further south there used to be a now rare **Bellman** and an **'A1' hanger** (both of which no longer exist) in the direction of Sinnington Road. Continuing around the curve of Master Road, the **1931 W & J.Riding hanger** already mentioned and the sole surviving elegant **'C' type** (now used by British Gas) form an arc, to the north of which was the **gymnasium and chancel** at the east end of Millbank Lane. At the end of Master Road turning west, along Millbank Lane, then southwards along Thornaby Road (the third side of the triangle) there are six brick built **AMQs** established in 1930 and 1933 (now in use as private residences). It was along here that **Thornaby Hall**, which was latterly used as a sick quarters and dental surgery with the coachman's house being used as a morgue, was surrounded by **barrack block accommodation, officer's mess** and **dining room** capable of catering for 761 WAAFs and airmen at each sitting. The residence of the **CO** (which is now called 'Cleveland Lodge') and **temporary officer accommodation** were located 100 yards further south. To the south east of the junction of Thornaby Road and Cunningham Road were the original **ATC camp huts**. The **watch office**, was located (at the end of Sinnington Road) some 250 yards south of the British Gas 'C' Type hanger, facing the **runways** and looking out towards the **bomb disposal** dumps located alongside Stainsby Beck in the south eastern part of the airfield. The larger dump was to the east of the site now used by Christ the King R.C school and the other dump was some one mile further south on land now part of Thornaby Industrial Estates. The **gunnery range** (MG Butts) was located midway between the two dumps to the east of the 'Cunningham Drive' perimeter track.

Parts of the **'Runways'** are still recognisable, having been incorporated into various road construction schemes. For those wishing to trace the original site of the runways refer to the **Map of Thornaby Aerodrome** on the last page then read on. The main NE/SW No.2 runway can be traced from the junction of Wolsingham Drive and Mitchell Avenue alongside Bassleton School playing fields, along Mitchell Avenue, through the 'Pavillion' in the town centre to join Trenchard Avenue, then across Thornaby Road to join Middleton Avenue in the south-west. Runway No.1 started in the north-west at the end of Trenchard Avenue, past the 'Golden Eagle Hotel' and through the 'Health Centre' to continue along Tedder Avenue and end at 'Stirling House'. The west east runway started from the east at Westlands School, across Tedder Avenue crossing open space past the end of Haviland Road, through the roundabout at Trenchard Avenue and Bader Avenue to continue along Bader Avenue and end alongside Bader Primary School.

Significant parts of **perimeter tracks** have also been absorbed into housing estates and bear street names such as Lingfield, Wolsingham, Yeadon, Middleton (behind the Harold Wilson Recreation centre) and Cunningham which is the most complete peri-track running east from Thornaby Road.

Perhaps it would have been better to have left the runways unaltered, in tribute to those pilots and crews who used them and who failed to endure the pitfalls of war, and allow others to walk along memory lane?

Bellman Hangers collapsed under the weight of snow during winter 1940/41.

THORNABY Aerodrome Expansion - Water tower constuction

THORNABY Airfield. Construction of Runway. 1939

THORNABY Aerodrome. Further expansion.

THORNABY Aerodrome. Buildings and Services take shape.

References

	21 Reservoir	86 Parachute Store
6 NAAFI & Sgts. Mess	TH Engine Test House	49 Armoury
TC Tennis Court	MG Firing Range	49 Photographic Sectn
10 Barrack Block	47 Main Store	50 MT Sheds & Yard
21 WT Mast	47 Workshops	61 SHQ - CO & Admin
21 Water Tower	42 Aero. Shed '29	c.1935

The Operations Block is used as a back cloth for ATC 1261 sdn. c1960.

A temporary timber hut at Thornaby Aerodrome. The sole survivor after 50 years. August 1992

Nr. E 453/40/080 Geogr. Lage: 1°17′30″ W, 54°32′ N. Höhe ü. d. M. 16 m Stand:
n. 3. 8. 40 Maßstab etwa 1:10 000 (1 cm = 100 m)

Flugplatz (AERODROME)
THORNABY
etwa 800 x 1000 m
GB 10 225

References
1 *12 Flugzeughallen* (Hangers) etwa 26,000 qm (sq.metres)
2 *2 Werft - u. Montagehallen* (Workshops) *etwa* 3,000 qm
3 *Unterkünfte* (A/Qtrs) *etwa* 10,000 qm
4 *Verwaltungs* (Admin.Bldg) -u. Betriebsgeb. *etwa* 6,000 qm
5 *Munitionslager* (Bomb Disposal area) *etwa* 1,000 qm
6 *3 Startbahner etwa* 850, 800, -u. 750 m
7 *Rollbahnen* (Perimeter)
8 *Abstellplätze* (Dispersals)
9 *Peilanlage* (Wireless Installn)
10 *Kleinkampfanlagen* (Fighter Pen)
11 *Flak - MG* (LAA)
12 *Schwere Flakstellung* (HAA)

INVADERS BEWARE

As the enemy persisted in its attempts to invade the airfield and surrounding area, so did the home defences gain in strength and effectiveness, as testified by those enemy aircrew who failed to return to their homeland alive.... some of whom lie buried in **Thornaby Cemetery**.

During the first year of hostilities, Thornaby airfield was defended by the 8th company of the **NDC** who were made up mostly from 'old soldiers' from the 1914 war who were officially recognised as a 'body' on 20 August 1939 under the jurisdiction of the **Green Howards** (later, in 1941 they were integrated into the Green Howards). **SPs** guarded the main gate. Guards, armed with WWI Lee Enfield rifles were mounted at aircraft dispersal points, to protect aircraft which were parked adjacent to the paths running alongside parts of the airfield, against sabotage by the **IRA** or other enemy sympathisers. Battalions of the 'Green Howards' and the 'Nottingham and Derbyshires' and then later the Royal Northumberland Fusiliers were responsible for the defence of RAF Thornaby and the training of RAF personnel stationed there in the use of weapons. As the threat of certain war seemed more ominous, additional trench shelters were constructed on the airfield to cope with extra auxiliary officers and airmen and by the time war had been declared all RAF station personnel had been trained to cope with any enemy gas attack. The surrounding area was protected by the military involving at one stage eight battalions of **LDVs** (rudely refered to as the Look, Duck and Vanish Brigade), who were formed on 15 May 1940 (later renamed **Home guards** on 23 July 1940).

At No.15 Balloon Centre head quarters, which was located in ICI main buildings until February 1941, when it moved to Hartburn Lodge in **Hartburn** Village, a **balloons barrage** was organised by **RAF 938 sdn** to discourage low level air attacks and force enemy bombers to drop their bombs less accurately from a higher altitude. The squadron consisted of four flights. Forty eight balloons covered Teesside area, 34 of which hovered over the industries and communications of this area, the remaining 14 covering the Middlesbrough Iron Masters area, Newport marshalling yards, South Bank and Grangetown. Each balloon was filled with 20,000 cu.ft of hydrogen gas and measured 66 feet long and 30 feet high and cost £25 to make. Accommodation, for what were locally recruited volunteers plus a few regular officers to form balloon crews, initially consisted of one hut plus latrine. This was later changed to three huts plus ablution blocks... the extra cost of having WAAFs replace male operators! Eventually balloons were mainly manned by **WAAFs** each of whom, after six weeks training as a Group Two trade received 2/4d to 6/8d per day according to rank.

On Saturday prior to the outbreak of war, on 2 September 1939 most of the barrage balloons were set on fire during an electric storm...the first of several such events. The **'Balloons Barrage'** was equipped with bleepers (radio warning devices to warn friendly aircraft) and was sited at various strategic points throughout the area. ICI Billingham was ringed by five balloons located at ICI works (at the East Gate, Plastic works Gate and South site Plastics works, Oxygen corner (to the east of), and North Gate; four at Belasis (at ICI Project store, Marlborough Road, Belasis Hall and off Greenwood Road); five in the Billingham area (at the bottom of Billingham Bank, the Recreation Ground next to the Green, Central Avenue, Mill Lane and Imperial Road); two at Norton Bottoms (N of Fleet Bridge Road and N of Fleet Road); two in Cowpen Lane (SE of Charltons Pond and N of the Railway Bridge) and one at the North Tees works Gate on Seal Sands. At Haverton Hill two balloons were located along Clay pits Road and at the Furness Shipyard site. At Port Clarence four were located at the Tar Distillation works and to the NE of the Tar works, along Seaton Carew Road and by the Riverside along the A1046 road. Two balloons were sited near Newport Bridge at Portrack Lane (near 'Dickens Hypermarket') and alongside the riverside at Dorman Long' works and two at Norton in Mount Pleasant and South Road and one in the St.Anns area (Tilery). At Thornaby two balloons were sited close to LNER marshalling yards and Head Wrightson River side area and one was located opposite Newtown School alongside Lustrum Beck off Bishopton Road in Stockton. The balloons barrage although designed to protect the many industries on Tees side caused many problems for Thornaby pilots. At times balloons had to be lowered to permit the longest runway to be used. On occasion balloons came away from the end of the cable attached to the balloon, due to bad weather conditions or misdirected shells from the ack-ack. Pilots obtained some useful gunnery practice shooting down wayward balloons. Local squadrons were officially credited with destroying several enemy aircraft but many raiders made contact with balloon cables which undoubtedly caused damage to their aircraft thereby affecting their chances of a safe return home. The usefulness of the barrage as a weapon is open to question, one source claimed that there were only five confirmed losses of enemy aircraft being brought down throughout the UK. Sadly it was often our own aircraft which were sometimes caught out by the barrage with somewhat tragic consequences. Local property or population also suffered due to trailing cables coming adrift and falling across streets, pavements, chimney stacks and church steeples.

The first **'Yellow Warning'** was received on 3 September 1939 at 11.40 hours and the 'White all clear' followed at 12.30 hours. alerts increased in frequency and duration in the days that followed.

During September 1939 decoy flare-paths were installed at **Middleton St.George.**

The **FIRST enemy aircraft** to be brought down on land in the United Kingdom was at Isle of Hoy on **17 October 1939** when Uffz.Ambrosius was captured and three other German airmen died and remain buried at Lyness in the Orkneys.

By 12 December 1939 all footpaths and bridle-paths in the vicinity of the airfield were closed to the public and marked with Police Notices which stated 'Right of way temporarily closed'. Amidst public outcry the CO decided to strengthen the perimeter defences by using **barbed wire** around the outside of the perimeter fence some of which overhung No.8 bus shelter, and exercised his right to close Thornaby Road. Much of the farm land beside the river was covered with barbed wire and the CO's house in Thornaby Road was barricaded. To placate protesting residents who claimed that the wire should be placed within the fence it was explained that the wire must be outside the fence, so as to prevent potential saboteurs or enemy airborne troops jumping over the fence. Thornaby Road residents living adjacent to the airfield requiring access had to show their passes although familiar faces freely walked past the sentry on duty.Regular chores for the average erk, complete with gas mask, included Black out Duty, Fire Duty, Picket Duty, Main Guard Duty, Hanger Key Duty and so many other duties. Dispersal Duty, especially with aircraft nicely placed for sabotage against a moonlight skyline ensured that many a night was going to be one of cap naps and tension for the average erk. Threats of action by the IRA led to the strengthening of the guard on duty each night at key points like the Armoury and hangers.

In December 1939 the RAF started to recruit and train **GGs.**

Because the RAF was stationed at Thornaby and local industry was geared up for war time production, it was expected that this area would be a priority target for the enemy, so extra equipment was allocated to the **ARP** ... schools were closed until air raid shelters were erected, road signs were removed, blackout imposed on houses and buildings, street lighting was turned off and motor vehicle lights were masked by shields with slits cut in them. Barricades blocked many roads leaving only enough space for a wagon to pass through. Thornaby Road was blocked off and mine traps prepared between Jolly Sailors and Hamiltons' Post Office. Road blocks were placed at the junction of Millbank Lane and Lovers Lane.

The complete **blackout** made walking very difficult. Many deaths caused by road traffic accidents during blackout, reduced as the effects of petrol rationing in 1940 affected the casual car user. The pedestrian was helped by the painting of black and white hoops and the use of 'glimmer' lighting on lamp posts in town centres and at road junctions and by the introduction of summer time and double summer time in the summer months to give extra daylight in the evenings.... During the war for every 11 civilians killed by enemy bombing, nine were killed in road accidents. Other civil Defence measures taken to counter the menace of invasion were varied... Long timber poles were erected in fields to prevent gliders from landing, tank traps, road side ditches and concrete 500lb cylinders were put in place, buses were wheel locked, all vehicles were immobilised when not in use, armed guards patrolled petrol garages and rifles were issued to police so as to apprehend paratroopers.... although according to one observer no special precautions were taken to protect the bomb dumps.

The fall of **Dunkirk on 4 June 1940** acted as a spur to speed up the building of inland lines of defence so that by late July 1940 pill boxes were all in position. Five pill boxes each crewed by four men were sited along the east side of Stainsby Beck to guard the easterly airfield perimeter. One hexagonal shaped box still remains behind Stainsby Riding School. Of the others one about 800 yards south was demolished by a building developer; another 800 yards north was removed by a farmer to make way for a new barn; another was buried underneath the Acklam Road/A174 Road Intersection and a fifth was lately removed from Bassledon School Playing Ground. Next to Thornaby Woods a rectangular pill box was sited near the East/West runway. At the top of Leven Bank four pill boxes gave extra cover to the south most runways; two at Cow Close Farm still over look River Leven Bridge; one lies alongside the Hilton road and another was sited a few yards north of the Half Moon Inn. Other gun points were strategically located inside the perimeter fencing and between the two main hangers.

By the fall of France, on 22 June 1940, the threat of invasion became a reality by which time barricades had been built around outlying parts of Thornaby village. At the end of Bassleton Lane (at the junction with the present day Bader Avenue), four Hispano guns were mounted on emplacements sited within the SW corner of the perimeter near Thorntree Farm. Prior to the 'Hispanos', LAA units deployed on the airfield were armed only with LMGs. All available transport on the airfield was armed. Lorries and 'Crossley' tenders were fitted with gun rings on which were mounted LMGs. Additional armament by way of four armoured vehicles from CMS works at Wolverhampton arrived during June 1940, which together with many of the improvised armed lorries and tenders were replaced by a fleet of Armadillo armoured vehicles during August. One guarded the main entrance and others carried out patrol duties. More LMGs were issued and quantities of rifles were issued to the Guard House and Operations Block. Gunnery practice, small arms drill and gas survival courses were of necessity carried out by all ranks. The Ground Defences were gradually strengthened by intakes of GGs. Each intake included 60 GG airmen each of whom were armed with a P14 WW1 rifle and had previously just completed two weeks training at Blackpool. Their task was to guard command posts, ammunition dumps and aircraft around the perimeter. By mid August the ground defence was well equipped with armoured vehicles and adequate ammunition. Adequate trench shelters had been installed around the airfield. Shelters for the public were mostly of the Anderson type. Each shelter consisted of two curved walls of corrugated steel which met via a ridge at the top and bolted to stout rails and sunk three feet into the ground and covered with eighteen inches of earth, although brick communal shelters for 50 people were also made.

The **7th AA** Division was responsible for **air defences** throughout the region which covered Leeds, Tees and Tyne and guns varied in number depending on availability and priorities. On 11 July 1940 the region had 118 HAA guns available for use including 14 for aerodromes. Vital points were also covered by 50 LAA and 321 Hispano and Lewis LMGs. Teesside was designated a HAA zone and 30 HAAs guns were allocated to the Tees area. Mostly Bofors, the guns were sited at key strong points to defend the **airfield:-** One was near the Half Moon Inn at Leven (now the Fox Covet); another along Low Lane (near the Post House Inn); one behind the Jolly Farmers' Inn down by the River Tees and another opposite Stockton race course. Elsewhere guns were sited to the **North of the airfield.** At the 'Two Mile House' in Durham Road, Stockton 4.5" ships guns were embedded in the field opposite 'Kiora' (off Rostrevor Avenue) and opposite the regional Ammuntion Depot (now a Co-op Hypermarket) along Blakeston Lane. Guns were also at the Birkdale Road junction with Darlington Road (to the west of) in Hartburn, Stockton just half a mile from Gunnery HQ at Elton; the junction of Portrack and Newport Bridge Road; the junction of Cowpen Bewley Road and Haverton Hill Road (near Davy United Roll Foundry); Pentland School playing field; Saltholme in Port Clarence and near Holme House Farm off Portrack Back Lane. At Billingham guns were sited at ICI main office block in Central Avenue and at the junction of Greenwood Road and Belasis Avenue in ICI sports fields. To the south sits wre based around Middlesbrough at Cold Knuckles Farm (now Brambles Farm); in the Rugby field off Green Lane; on the old

Golf Course at Saltersgill; Tree Bridge Corner and near Poole Hospital along the Great Ayton to Nunthorpe Road. Later, Z Rocket launchers each capable of firing sixty four 4" diameter six feet long rockets simultaneously, were installed. Two were in use. One on Portrack marshes not far from Newport Bridge and one at Saltersgill.

The port and harbour defences for **Hartlepool and the Tees** consisted of one 9.2" built in 1918 at Coatham, six 6" (two at the Heugh; two at Coatham and two at Seaton), and two 12 pounder guns on Middleton Pier Hartlepool. Later one fixed 6" gun was sited at Port Clarence and much later a US 4.7" ack-ack gun was sited at South Gare.

Searchlights units were installed at suitable stategic locations related to AA sites. Each searchlight detachment consisted of one commander, two spotters (remote), a sound locator team of one locator and two listeners, a generator operator, searchlight operator and long arm elevator operator and cook. One searchlight unit was sited opposite Cowley House Farm off Durham Lane and another on Elton Moor not far from the Sutton Arms in Elton. Evidence of searchlight sites still remain at Baysdale Abbey and at Sledale Beck off the Kildale/Commondale Road. Unless the Luftwaffe flew below 12,000 feet or on cloudless nights, searchlights were mostly ineffective and when enemy aircraft flew at over 20,000 feet in order to avoid flak during night raids the target areas were lit up by searchlights.

The 3" Bofors guns which were effective only up to 25,000 feet were later supported by high altitude 4.5" (ex Navy) and 3.7" guns effective up to 45,000 feet. The heaviest guns sited north of the River Tees were the 4.5" static guns based near Kiora which when fired deafened nearby residents. Much heavier guns used for coastal defences existed in the UK such as the 18" rail mounted 'Bockbuster' or 15" busty strip cartoon 'Jane' and 14" 'Winnie and Pooh's.

The **Royal Observer Corps** armed with plotting instruments, sound locators and binoculars, set up thirteen observation posts throughout Teesside as part of York No.9 group. One post was sited at Eaglescliffe on the Golf Course. and another at Seaton Carew. Others were at West Hartlepool and Newton Bewley behind the 'Blue Bell' and at Saltburn, Redcar, Eston, Loftus, Great Ayton and Osmotherly. The posts were on higher ground and were manned at all times by two men, (or sometimes women as from July 1941). Each pair completed a four hour watch whose job it was to ensure the accurate visual identification of all aircraft, both friend and foe overflying their specific area. Once an aircraft was seen or heard it's position was plotted and communicated by ROC to other posts and aerodrome operations rooms and AA Command via **No.13 Fighter Command HQ**. In conjunction with radar reports the accurate locations of all aircraft were known. Air raid warning 'Red Alerts' from ROC posts were distributed via the **National Air Raid Centre** at Middlesbrough throughout the region which gave five minute warning of an imminent air raid. 'Purple Alert' signified lights out but no alert. The sighting of a single fighter or reconnaissance aircraft was not sufficient to warrant a 'Red Alert'.... Very often useful information could be obtained for 'Y' Service (who succeeded in decoding the enemy secret code 'Enigma' by late 1940) by listening into enemy radio frequencies. The ROC also assisted in the direction and location of **crashed aircraft** for ambulance and rescue vehicles. The ROC also kept watch for enemy troopships, glider landings and para-troops whilst naval vessels cleared enemy mines away from our beaches.

As early as May 1940 until August 1940 **Radar** was secretly installed around the north east coast. **Danby Beacon** was disguised as an oil rig complete with tankers so as to complete the illusion. Closely guarded by RAF, Danby Beacon (CH Chain Home), Staxton Wold (CH), and CHLs (Chain home low) at Bamburgh, Shotton, Flamborough and Easington, were able to forewarn **RAF Thornaby** of the presence of enemy aircraft over 100 miles away. The inter relationship between ROC and Radar was absolutely essential so as to successfully determine aircraft identification, position and height prior to action being taken by **No.13 Fighter Command** from their under ground HQ at Kenton Bar, Newcastle.

The **FIRST bombs dropped on German soil** were by thirty Whitleys and twenty Hampdens of **77 sdn** Driffield. On **19 March 1940** the Isle of Sylt was attacked in retaliation for the attack on the Orkneys on **16 March 1940** when the **FIRST civilian Mr. Jim Ibister** was killed. This raid preceded the

FIRST mainland attacks on Munchen Gladbach on the night of 11/12 May 1940.

The **FIRST** raid on Italy, also by 77 sdn, took place on the night of 11/12 June 1940 on the Fiat factories at Turin

Air raids on Cargo Fleet and South Bank on **25 May 1940** resulted in the **FIRST civilian** casualties in mainland Britain, then on 4 June 1940 a Heinkel 111 of KG26 dropped four bombs on Billingham Bottoms and severely damaged Norton Mill.

On the night of **5/6 June 1940** Thornaby airfield was bombed and two **Hudsons** (N7309 and P5157) were destroyed whilst being filled with fuel and two Bowsers destroyed. The enemy aircraft followed the runway lights whilst pilots were training. Six bombs were dropped alongside the runway. Regardless of danger Commanding Officer (CO) G/C.Simpson refused shelter until all personnel were safely sheltered. Even so one airman was killed and a policeman was injured. These bombs were the first heard in the vicinity of the airfield. The explosion caused everybody to instinctively grab whatever was to hand, be it a rifle or pick handle, whilst struggling into suitable dress. Alarms happened on the next two nights. On the second night after a thorough search two UXBs were found.

Air raids averaged two per day during this period and the talk was that 'Thornaby was in for it!'... Security precautions intensified. On 9 July 1940 it was decided to evacuate every body living within a thousand yards from the airfield if the situation justified such action. Such action was never taken. Intense German air activity continued throughout 1940 and orders were given that all personnel should be ready for enemy attacks at all times. The Spitfire mkIs of 41 and 54 fighter squadrons at **RAF Catterick**, some of which were detached to Greatham, were generally responsible for the seeking out and elimination of enemy aircraft attacking Thornaby and the surrounding area which extended north to the Wear and south to Whitby. Fighter squadrons at **Usworth** and **Acklington** also assisted in giving cover against enemy attack when circumstances permitted.

Defence preparations at Thornaby were reasonably complete by the time the Battle of Britain started.

One of the **FIRST attacks** on this area resulted in the crew of a HeIII of 2/KG4 being lost at sea off **Blyth** whilst on a sortie to **Middlesbrough on 27 June 1940**. A few days later, whilst mine-laying off the Tees, Fw200C-1 F8+EH of 2/KG40 was shot down, probably by ack-ack fire, and crashed into the sea off **Crimdon Dene** at 23.55 hours on 19 July 1940. Four of the crew of six crew, Hptmn.Stesszyn, Fwbl.Meier and Gefrs.Zaunig and J.Perl perished. Two others Fwbl.Kulkem and Fwbl.Nicolai were captured and taken POW.

Nasty accidents sometimes happened.... or nearly happened. During one air raid during the spring of 1940 at 6.00 hours, the station sirens sounded and everyone headed for the underground shelters. One airman, after a night out at the Royal Hotel, could scacely believe his own eyes. A **Wellington** bomber whilst being guided in to make a safe landing by a Spitfire and Blenheim, was fired on by perimeter Ack-ack Guns and threatened by Ground defence men with bayonets at the ready on top of their make shift Armoured Vehicle. The aircraft had been mistaken for an enemy bomber escorted by our fighters! Aircraft spotting was sometimes not so good with ack-ack guns mistakenly opening fire even though the friendly recognition signal had been given. During late 1940, at dawn in thick fog, one mobile column had the misfortune to shunt into another whilst patrolling the airfield and caused serious injury to one airman.

During early 1940 day time nuisance raids persisted. Barrage balloons were shot down and dummy parachutes were dropped by the enemy. As enemy attacks developed during the day, a war of nerves persisted. **Ack-ack priority** was to protect aircraft when most vulnerable... at take off and landing as calls on local squadron fighter ever increased. Resources of army ack-ack were strained and were necessarily supplemented by detachments from RAF who operationally directed the ack-ack from **Fighter HQ**, although the ack-ack still came under the command of the 7th AA division.

The official British version of the **Battle of Britain** lasted from 10 July until 31 October 1940. The job of Luftwaffe 5, which was based in Aalborg in Denmark and Stavenger in Norway with HQ in Oslo was to wipe out the home defences in the Tyne Tees area after airfields in southern England had been eradicated. On 9 August 1940 HeIIIH-3 1H+ER of 7/KG26, was shot down by F/L.R.F.H.Clerke, Sgt.J.Wright and P/O.G.H.Nelson-Edwards in three Hurricanes of **79 sdn** from **Acklington**, and crashed into the sea off **Whitburn** at 11.52am after dumping bombs on Sunderland. The crew of Uffz.Karkos and Feirekat were both wounded and Uffz.O.Denmer and Fw.W.Haertel were rescued by a naval patrol boat. Two days later a Ju88A-1 7A+KH of 1F/121 at 7.08am whilst on a reconnaissance sortie over the moors around Ugthorpe at **Mickleby** (near Whitby) was shot down by F/O.Boyle, Sgt.E.V.Darling and P/O.Wallens in **Spitfires** of **41 sdn** from RAF Catterick. Of the crew of four Lt.Heinrich Meier, killed due to gunshot wounds, lies buried in **Thornaby cemetery,** and Fw.O.Hofft, Oblt.H.Marzusch and Fw.K.Hacker were captured. The heaviest ever day attack during this period, in the Teesside area, took place two days after Hitler declared an all out offensive against the RAF on 'Adler Tag' (Eagle Day) on 13 August 1940 .... **'A Day to Remember!** 'briefly recounts actions of **15 August 1940.**

The high losses inflicted on both aircraft and crews of the Luftwaffe on that day forced the enemy to change tactics regarding further mass daytime attacks on the North East. On 20 August 1940 a Ju88 A-1 aircraft sortied to attack **Thornaby airfield** was shot down by Hurricanes of 302 sdn at 7.10pm at Partington near Hull. Two crew members Uffz.W.Rautenburg and two days later Obfw.W.H.Kruczinski both died and two others Uffz.F.G.Wollf and Fw.H.Keller survived to tell the tale. The Luftwaffe targeted night attacks on **Thornaby airfield** and other military installations and factories at Stockton, Billingham, Hartlepool and Middlesbrough on **24 August 1940**. Apart from ICI Billingham, where heavy bombing caused serious damage to a pipe bridge and silos no other target was hit although tragically a girl was killed at **Grangetown**. This was the same night, when a Luftwaffe pilot lost his way and unintentionally bombed civilians in densely populated London. This incident triggered off previously planned retaliation raids by the RAF to be made against Berlin using Hampden and Wellington bombers. Ten Berlin civilians were killed on 28 August 1940. Hitler decreed on 4 September 1940 that the Luftwaffe switch tactics away from primarily destroying airfields to blitzing the civilian population.

Attacks on airfields were effectively restricted to 'tip and run raids'.This change in tactics undoubtedly saved many of our airfields from being non-operational during the Battle of Britain and contributed to the postponement of the **invasion of England** (operation code name 'Sealion') on 20 September 1940 and the ultimate cancellation on 16 January 1941. In the event of invasion being imminent, contingency plans existed to use 'shadow squadrons' of OTU trainee fighter pilots and instructors to defend southern England and for the OTUs of coastal command squadrons (including **Hudsons at Thornaby**) to take on a fighter role as defenders of other areas of Britain. The **'Marquis'**, nicknamed the 'Hedgehogs'were formed to specialise in unarmed combat and sabotage. They would emerge from cells discretely hidden around the countryside, at places like Bishopton, Eston, Wynyard and Roseberry Topping to combat any invading force. They were like the 'Y' service a very secret service.

On 25 August 1940 at Thornaby, Victoria Bridge was damaged. During the Battle of Britain attacks continued on many airfields in Yorkshire and Durham, mine-laying operations continued in the Tees area and daytime reconnaissance missions persisted. On 24 September 1940 during an air raid at 05.00 hours on **Thornaby airfield** a bomb penetrating 30 feet deep before exploding.

By mid August 1940 the Germans had invented **'Knickerbein'** which was a beam guidance system designed to guide enemy bombers to their target with minimal navigable help and was known to be used to locate aircraft factories. Radio counter measures re-radiated the beams transmitted, so as to misguide enemy raiders, by erecting a series of masked beacons (Meacons) manned by former radio hams recruited by RAF 'Y' service.

As a result of battle experience gained the **airfield defence** system was changed. GGs were in charge of four inner gun posts each manned by crew of five men using US type machine guns. Four men plus two Lewis guns were allocated to protect the operations room. Hispano AA posts were reorganised and better equipment was made available such as Hotchkins machine guns and armour piercing bullets. An airman with Lewis gun could be observed on patrol on top of the 70feet high water tower. The ground defence section had an establishment of around 350 GGs, some of whom were attached to Greatham for several weeks at a time. The GGs mostly manned the various defence posts inside the airfield but on occasion patrolled the perimeter. One Scotsman well recollects the need for a brace of rum after one such two hour patrol during the bitterly cold winter of 1940/41. In the event of attack the defence of the airfield was controlled from the Battle HQ stronghold sited mostly below the ground apart from a six feet square observation post projecting three feet above the ground. Battle HQ liased with army gunnery control at **Elton Hall**.

During November 1940 the **FIRST ever civilian QL and QF decoy** night sites in the U.K were installed on Teesside at ICI (8 sites) and Dorman Long (2 sites) to complement the **decoy airfield** manned by 24 airmen built near **Grangetown** between Lazenby village and the trunk road, (now part of the ICI Wilton complex). This 'Dummy' airfield (K site) was complete with full size dummy Blenheims, lorries, control tower, gun placements and airfield buildings to which was added a Q site consisting of a flare-path and circuit lights so as to resemble **Thornaby airfield**. The `spoof' was not noticeable from the nearby main A1085 road. Another Q site was operated by 2 men at **Middleton St.George** (referred to as Goosepool - now known as Teesside International Airport) until 15 January 1941 when it was used as an airfield by **78 sdn** with **Whitley mkV** bombers. Another Q site was at Low Field Farm off the Hilton/Seamer Road, complete with lights, generator, control equipment and underground bunker which were regularly used and a grate filled with creosoted timber which was never lit. Remains still exist of a bunker on the ICI Q site built by Elstree Studios and manned by ICI staff at Smith House Farm at Elton. By mid June 1942, enemy rconnaissance had identified many of the Dummy Daytime K airfield sites and only three UK sites remained in use. By the end of 1944 all dummy QF and QL decoy night sites were closed down. As to the value of dummy sites, it was officially estimated that dummy K and Q airfields were hit the same number of times as real airfields and that seven times as many HE bombs dropped on them as on operational airfields.

During 1940/41 apart from concentrations of bombs on London, some experienced enemy crews carried out night raids on aircraft factories and airfields often during poor weather conditions, thereby gaining the element of surprise. Many enemy airmen failed to survive the journey across the North Sea in search of airfields, industry and other targets in our area. Many, apart from being shot down by the diligent fighter pilots of **RAF Catterick, Usworth and Acklington**, ack-ack fire, coastal guns or maybe warship were beaten by the weather or mechanical failure. Not only did prominent industrial towns suffer from enemy attacks. On 6 November 1940 **Northallerton** was attacked and four bombs were dropped near **Marske** railway station and one person was killed. By 1941, the North East coast was very well defended so much so that German pilots called Teesside **'Hell's Corner'**. Nevertheless air raids persisted until 22 March 1943.

On 30 March 1941, Ju88A (0115) 4U+GH of If/123 (part of Field Marshall Sperrle's Luftflotte 3 in France (near Paris) was on a reconnaissance mission to Manchester. At 3.50pm it was shot down by F/L.A.D.J.Lovel DFC of **41 sdn** from **RAF Catterick** and dived into **Barnaby Moor, near Eston**. The aircraft was abandoned and the crew of Lt.Wolfgang Scloth (pilot), Lt.Otto Meinhold (Ob), Fw.Willi Schmigale (WOp) and Uffz.Hans Steigerwald (F.Eng/AG) were all killed. The latter named lies buried in **Thornaby cemetery**

Enemy Bomber units operated from Holland during 1941 to 1943 and attacked shipping and other strategic targets. Mostly 500kg HE bombs and ICs were used. During the spring of 1941 this area suffered heavy bombing when the Luftwaffe was at the peak of its' power. During one raid alone on 15 April 1941 it was estimated that 100 enemy aircraft attacked North east targets. On 4/5 May Hartlepool was attacked by 20 aircraft which dropped 28 tons of HE bombs followed by 20 aircraft and 32 tons of HE bombs the next night. On the last night of the 'Blitz on London' on 11 May 1941 nineteen aircraft dropped 27 tons of HE bombs on Hartlepool on Lumley Square (12 people killed), Stockton (eight people killed) and ICI Billingham.

In the ensuing months, this area continued to be attacked both day and night as did London and elsewhere in UK, even though enemy aircraft available were severely depleted due to the invasion by Hitler of Russia. On 3/4 June 1941 JU88c-2 (0570) R4+LK crashed into a hill on **Skelder Moor near Whitby** in bad visibility at 12.30am. All the crew were killed. Lt.Johannes Feuerbaum, Obgefr.Rudolf Peters and Gerhard Deenzer lie buried in **Thornaby cemetery**. During the same month other enemy aircraft were known to have crashed into cliffs along the North Yoorkshire coast due to fog.

On 8 August 1941 a Hudson hit the cable of the balloon sited in **Albert Park**. Fortunately it was able to land safely as indeed was a Whitley bomber based at Middleton St.George after colliding with a balloon cable above the Head Wrightson riverside site.

Saltburn was attacked and the Flying Scotsman was machine gunned at **Berwick-on-Tweed** on 1 November 1941 during daylight hours. Ack-ack fire from HMS Quantock shot down JU88 (1409) of 2/KfGp.506 which crashed into cliffs at 5.40 pm during that same day at **Ravenscar**. The crew of four were either killed or missing. Ob.f-zur see Karl Scultz, the pilot of that ill-fated enemy aircraft, Obfw.Werner Hanel and an UNKNOWN German, (who is probably one of the other two crew Oblt.Weber (Staf Kapt) or Uffz.A.Grabrlie) both of whom were reported missing), lie buried in **Thornaby cemetery**.

On 15 January 1942 **Billingham Balloon** barrage caught Dornier Do217E-4 (5314) U5+HS of 8/KG2 whilst mine laying. The plane hit the cable and dived on to a railway line at **South Bank** at 6.20pm killing the crew of four, Uffz.H.Manecke, Fw.Joachim Lehris, Obfw.H.Richter and Lt.R.Matern. The latter three lie buried in **Thornaby cemetery**. Yet during a raid on ICI Billingham and Haverton on 8 July 1942 enemy bombers flew through the same barrage. One aircraft touched the cable. Some WAAF balloon operators were injured by blast from bombs dropped nearby.

By early 1942 GGs numbers were much reduced, due to overseas needs, and only one armoured vehicle complete with Hispano cannon remained at **Thornaby airfield**. 'Tip and run' raiders evaded the efforts of the ROC by using lone raider fighter bombers which appeared out of the blue at low level and attacked sea side towns.

On the night when the oil tanks at ICI were set alight, on 6/7 July 1942 twenty enemy aircraft raided Teesside. IC bombs preceded by pre-raid parachute flare markers to illuminate the target area were thought to be dropped on **Thornaby airfield**. One such parachute was found hanging over a hanger door. On the following night 7/8 July a Do217 crashed off the Dutch coast when returning from a raid on Teesside and Do217E-4(4270) U5+BT was shot down by Beaufighters of **406 sdn** of **RCAF Scorton** and crashed into sea off **Middlesbrough**. The aircraft and crew of Oblt.G.Lanz, Fw.E.Jors, Uffzs.A.Engler and J.Klatt were lost.

Ironically, on 28 August 1942 at 11.04pm Ju88 A-4 (144146) crashed into the sea off **Sunderland** after being shot down by a Beaufighter VI of **406 sdn** of **RCAF Scorton** crewed by P/O.F.G.Harding and F/L.J.R.B.Frith, who were both killed when their plane, having lost one engine, crashed into a farm house at **Scorton**. Two of the four Junkers crew, Obfw.A.Riedal and Uffz.J.Pfeffer who was injured, baled out, and were taken POW. The other two were killed and were found three days later. Obfw.Paul Kalodzie was found at **Crimdon Dene** and Gefr.Josef Sander at **Blackhall Rocks**, both of whom are buried in **Thornaby cemetery**.

P/O.Perrin in a Typhoon mk1b of **1 sdn** from **RAF Acklington** shot down Me 210A-1 (2342) of 16/KG6, which was new to operations over England and was identified and tracked by local ROC observers whilst on an experimental sortie over Teesside. It crashed at Fell Briggs, **New Marske** on 6 September 1942 at 11.43am. Both crew members, Fw.H.Mosges and Ob.gefr.Edmund Czerny (Austrian) baled out but were killed when their parachutes failed to open and are buried in **Thornaby cemetery**. Me210s had an unsuccessful start to operations over England, one squadron by the end of the month had lost half of their aircraft.

Gradually enemy operating strength during 1942 dwindled from around 80 to 20 crews and sometimes reserves and trainee instructors were of necessity used. Enemy missions disguised routes to deceive night fighters and defences, using Path-finder crews of KG2. Nevertheless many enemy planes ventured across the North Sea only to fall victim to the **natural fortress** of the North Yorkshire moors, as did Dornier217E-4 (4342) U5=GR of 7/KG on 17 December 1942 which crashed at Crows Nest six miles NW of **Helmsley** at 10.15pm with the total loss of crew Oblt.R.Haussner (staf.Kapt), Uffz.S.Erd and Obfws.H.Hupe and E.Weiderer.

Dornier Do217E-4 (5441) U5+BL crewed by Oblt.E.Schneider (injured) and Uffz.M.Hoffmann (injured) and Uffz.J.Weber and Obfz.G.Eilbrecht, whilst held in searchlight was shot down by F/L.J.E.Wilson and F/O.D.C.Bunch in a Beaufighter of **219 sdn** from **RAF Scorton**, during a raid on **Thornaby**. The Dornier crew all baled out and were taken POW. The plane crashed at **Great Stainton** at 11.25pm on 11 March 1943. Douglas Kaye, a Canadian pilot, stationed at Thornaby, whilst taking his girl home from the Maison de Dance was witness to the devastation caused and observed that the danger encountered along Thornaby Road on that night was worse than anything suffered during night bombing raids. This same pilot was killed a few days later when his aircraft crashed on Bowesfield Farm, Stockton. His brother Keith, a soldier, visited the graves of his brother and comrades at Thornaby cemetery a few days before going to action on D Day.

Enemy mine-laying continued along Tyne-Tees coast and after the **LAST raid** on Redcar and the Hartlepools on 22 March 1943, two Dorniers of KG2 failed to return to base. Two months later F/O.Keele and F/O.Cowles in a Beaufighter of **604 sdn** from **RAF Scorton** shot down Do 217K-1 (4584) U5+DP which crashed in the sea thirty five miles east of **Sunderland** at 2.15pm on 17 May 1943. Two crew members Uffzs.Mittelstadt and Roos from the enemy plane were recovered from the sea, the latter named being buried in **Thornaby cemetery** on 2 July 1943 after being washed ashore at Blackhall Rocks. Two other crew Obgefr.G.Kaber and Uffz.A.Richter were missing.

By D Day there were so many troops stationed in Britain that it was said that the only thing that kept the island afloat was the multitude of airborne barrage balloons. Towards the end of 1944 as the risk of conventional air raids had diminished, barrage balloons were no longer really necessary and sites were gradually dismantled. Camouflage operations stopped in August 1944 and defence positions were abandoned during October 1944. On Early Xmas Eve 1944 at 6.05 am our one and only experience of **flying bombs** occurred. Out of 40 Vls aimed at Manchester, 12 probably dropped in the sea and 28 were reported sighted. Of the 28 sightings seven were reported in Yorkshire and one in County Durham at **Tudhoe** after having passed over Billingham. These Vls were attached to He111s and launched in mid air at about 200 mph from a height of 500 metres by the flight engineer who started the Vl motor. Each missile had a range of 150 to 200 miles in addition to the 400 mph of the He111. The **LAST Vl** to approach UK was shot down by Ack-ack off Oxfordness on 29 March 1945 at 12.43pm.

Shortly before the arrival of the last V1, on the night of 4 March 1945 the little known **Giesela** raids took place when about one hundred enemy aircraft including Arado jet fighters mingled with allied planes returning from Rhineland raids. The only Free French bomber base in the UK, at Elvington near York, was severely attacked, Halifax NR229 whilst diverted to Croft airfield was shot down at 2.14am and crashed at **Hurworth**. Another Halifax and a further two Free French Halifax bombers were shot down at **Elvington** and a Ju88G-6 (620028) D5+AX intruder crashed at **Sutton-on-Derwent** after mistaking car head lights for aircraft lights on the runway at Elvington. All told four Mosquitos and nineteen allied bombers were lost although overall German losses were much heavier. A similar action on the following night resulted in more Allied night fighters being lost and on 17 March 1945 one more allied bomber was lost.

Oddly, even during the early war year some RAF Thornaby based personnel have no recollections of enemy action and need to take shelter. **How effective** a deterrent were the defences of Teesside against the enemy may be judged by the relatively low losses in industrial production and the minimal damage to **Thornaby** and **Greatham Airfields** caused by enemy air raids and those enemy aircrew who failed to survive after their mission to **Teesside**?

A Pill box which is now used as a hen house at Stainsby Riding School. 1991

A plume of smoke rises from the crash site of a Ju88 as shown by this aerial photograph taken by a Hudson of 220 sdn near Eston.   30 March 1941.

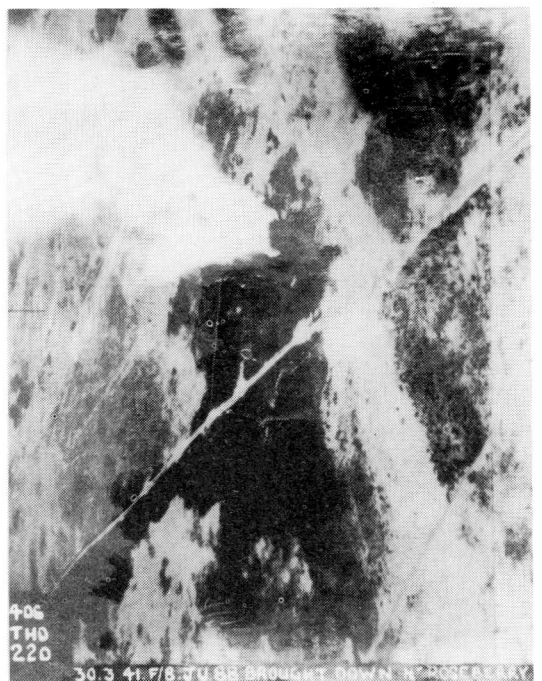

The grave of an UNKNOWN German Airman in THORNABY Cemetery.

CRASHES AND CEMETERIES

They came, they saw and for some they did not conquer........ not only Teesside, but the nearby areas of Wearside, Tyneside and North Yorkshire. Whilst on reconnaissance missions or operations involving flights which crossed over these areas or attacks on the area, several enemy aircraft were destined never to return to their homeland. Some crews became POWs but crews from many of these aircraft lie buried in the **War Graves** plots at **Thornaby** alongside many allied airmen who lost their lives during wartime operations or accidents in the air in the vicinity of Teesside.

The **FIRST** Germans to be CAPTURED on English soil were Uffzs. Bernhard Hochstuhl (wireless operator) and Eugen Lange (pilot) whilst on a reconnaissance mission to locate HMS Hood in the Firth of Forth, in a Heinkel 111 was shot down by three Spitfires of **41** sdn from **Catterick** and ditched in the sea twenty five miles from **Whitby** on 17 October 1939. Lange and Hochstuhl, though injured survived and were rescued from their dinghy at dawn next day. One crew member Lt. Kretchmer was missing and the body of Uffz. Saver was washed ashore on 30 October 1939 at Whitby.

The **FIRST** German aircraft to be SHOT DOWN on English soil crashed with bombs still on board two miles north of **Whitby** at 9.40am on 3 February 1940 and was guarded by personnel from RAF Thornaby. The site is now marked by a plaque at Bannial Flat Farm. Heinkel He111 (2323) 1H+FM of KG26 Gruppe was shot down by three Hurricanes from **43** sdn based at **Acklington**, one of which was piloted by G/C. Peter Townsend (famous in the 1950s because of a love affair with Princess Margaret). The crew of Fw. H. Wilms (kapitan), Uffz. R. Leuschake and Uffz. K. Missy who lost a leg and was later exchanged for an allied POW in 1943, were taken POW. Uffz. J. Meyer died from gunshot wounds. On the same day the crew of Lt. L von Bruning, Fws. H. Panzlaff and H. Peterson and Uffz. W. Penishke of Heinkel He111 1H+HL of 3/KG26 were all recovered (except Fw. Peterson who was missing) from **Druridge Bay** off the Northumberland Coast. They were shot down by F/Os. J.D. Edmonds and J.W.C. Simpson of **43** sdn. At 11.15am Hurricanes of 43 sdn were again in action some fifteen miles east of Tynemouth when He111H-3 1H+GK of 2/KG26 was shot down and crashed into the sea. Three of the crew, Obfw. F. Wiemer, Fw. F. Schnee and Uffz. H. Dietrich were captured. Uffz. W. Wolff was killed and Uffz. K-E. Thiede was taken from the sea and buried at **Grimsby**.

Acklington squadrons were alerted to enemy attacks as far north as the Tweed. A He115 float plane was shot down by fighters in bad weather off the **north east coast** on 30 June 1940. Next day a He111H-3 of 7/KG26 was shot down by three Hurricanes of **79** sdn from **Acklington** and crashed into the sea off **Tynemouth**. At 6.15am Heinkel HE59 D-ASAM displaying Red Cross markings of Seenotflug. Kdo on 1 July 1940 was shot down by Spitfires of **72** sdn from Acklington and crashed into the sea eight miles east of **Sunderland** and was beached. The crew of Lt. H-J. Fehske, Obgefr. E. Philipp and Uffzs. E.O. Ielen and Stuchmann who was wounded were all rescued from their dinghy by the Royal Navy.

During the mass attack by the Luftwaffe on **North East England** on 15 August 1940, during the **Battle of Britain**, many enemy aircraft were shot down or went missing but enemy attacks continued and so did casualties. On the night of 5 September 1940 He111P (3065) 5J+5P of 6/KG26, was shot down by ack-ack fire at 11.18pm and crashed on Suffolk Street in **Sunderland** killing the crew of Oblt. Schroder, Uffz. Reitz, Obgefr. Marten and Gefr. Wick all of whom are buried in **Hylton** cemetery. On the same day Heinkel He111 (6896) 1H+BC of 2/KG26 was shot down near the coast with the loss of all the crew of Uffz. Stenzel, Obfw. Vetter, Fw. Wilde and Obgefr. Wart. Next day the crew of Uffzs. Bartels and Schweizer, Obfw. Staffeldt, Fw. Markuse and Gefr. Meier of Heinkel He111H-3 (3258) 1H+HP of 6/KG26 failed to return from a sortie on **Sunderland**. An unusual incident witnessed on 16 September 1940 was the towing into **Eyemouth** Harbour of He115C (3261) 54+CL of 3/506K Flg which ditched in the sea seven miles north of **Berwick** due to engine failure probably caused by ack-ack fire. The Heinkel had been carrying out a torpedo attack on a convoy. The crew of Hptmn. E-W. Bergmann (Staf Kapitan), Oblt. Lucas, Fw. E.E. Kalinowski and Hptmn. H. Kriependorf were rescued from their dinghy by a fishing boat and taken as POWs.

Airfields were often under attack. Junkers Ju88A-5 (6129) 5J-ER of 7/KG4 was hit by ground fire during a low level attack on **Linton-on-Ouse** airfield at 6.00pm on 27 October 1940. The aircraft crashed at Richmond Farm near **Duggleby**. All the crew except Uffz.Piontek who was injured and later died, survived the crash and were captured. Staf Kapitan Oblt.Padbbielski, Uffz.Heier, and Uffz.Jidrawski became POWs. Linton was again attacked a few days later at 5.45pm on 1 November 1940 when Ju88A-1 (7089) 4D+TS of 8/KG30 flew into a hill at **Glaisdale Head** about 13 miles SW from Whitby, during bad visibility en route to the target of **Linton-on-Ouse** airfield. The crew of four, Uffzs.Wilhelm Woweriet, Alfred Rodermond and Gerhard Pohling and Obfw.Hans Shulte-Mater, were all killed and lie buried in **Thornaby Cemetery**.

Some of the most unlikely vessels were required for use by the Royal Navy, one of which was **HMS Southsea**, a paddle driven mine sweeper, which shot down Ju88A-5 (4026) F6+HL of 3(F)/122, on 17 November 1940 at 8.45am, which crashed into the sea off **Whitburn** near Sunderland. The crew of Lt.P.Thallmaier, Fw.A.Loise and Uffz.P.Hippenstiel were missing and Uffz.H.Maisbaum was killed.

On 6 January 1941, the 500th day of war the world famous aviator **Amy Johnson** drowned after she parachuted into the Thames estuary from an Airspeed Oxford which she was ferrying from **Blackpool**. Lt.Commander Walter Fletcher of the naval trawler Haslemere lost his life in a vain rescue bid.

The varying fortunes of war can be judged by some episodes which happened. A crash caused by colliding with a barrage balloon was not a regular event, yet He111P-4 (3085) 5J+GP did just that after being hit by ack-ack fire at Bents Park in South Shields on 16 February 1941. It dived to the ground, later exploded and caused the deaths of one policeman and three firemen. Four crew Hptmn.H.Styra, Uffz.KG.Brutzman and H.Seckstadt, and Gefr.F.Janeschitz were killed. The fifth crew man Obfw.W.Beetz was electrocuted after successfully baling out only to land on trolley bus wires.

Ju88A-5 (2234) MZ+JL of 3/Kust.flr Grp.106 was shot down by F/L.D.Sheen in a Spitfire of **72** sdn on 13 March 1941 at 10.25pm and crashed into the sea off **Amble**. The crew of Lt.zur see.R.Dietze, Obgefr.Wesseres and Obgefr.H.Vandanne and Oblt.Vorgtlander-Tetzer were missing except for the latter named whose body was washed ashore one mile south east of the Heugh light house at **Hartlepool** on 27 April 1941 and was buried in **Thornaby** cemetery on 1 May 1941.

72 sdn from **Acklington** again scored a hit on 10 April 1941 when Sgts.Casey and Prytherch shot down Ju88A-5 (0529) FL+NL of 3(F)/122 which crashed at **Alnmouth** during a reconnaissance mission to **Newcastle**. The crew of Lt.R.Braose, Uffz.E.Helmert and Fw.K.Daux were missing and the body of Fw.B.Graobkes was found at Amble. A week later on 16 April 1941 at 2.00am, the crew of He111H-5 (9370) A1+AL of 3/KG53 whilst on route to attack Belfast abandoned their aircraft due to engine failure. All the crew Ober.fw.Laekner, Hptmn.W.Horing (Staf Kapitan), Fws.K.Menzel and A.Wachter and Uffz.O.Seltmann baled out and were taken POWs. The aircraft dived into the ground at Bull Lane Bridge in **Huby** near Ripon. During the same month He111H-5 (3677) 1H+MH was shot down by gun fire whilst attacking fighter catapult ship **'Patia'**. Cdr.DMB.Baker went down with his ship which was damaged during this action at 9.30pm on 27 April 1941 about 35 miles off the Tyne. All the Heinkel crew except Gefr.J.Schurgel who was killed, of Obfw.Fenchel,Gefr.R.Klamand and Uffz.S.Warko baled out and were taken POW. During a sortie to **Whitley Bay** on 30 April 1941 Ju88A-1 (0715) S4+JH of 1/506 crashed off **Farne Islands** after being shot down by Spitfire of **72** sdn. The crew of Lt.H.Jack, Fw.K.Pahnke, Uffz.J.Schaare were all killed and Obgefr.J.Schumacher was taken from the sea. A Defiant flown by F/O Day of **141** sdn from Acklington shot down Ju88A-5 (7177) 4D+EN 5/KG30 which force landed on the north side of **Holy Island** at 4.00am on 7 May 1941. The aircraft was destroyed by the crew of Uffz.H.Schaber, Gefr.H.Noske, Fw.P.Graupner and Gefr.W.Arndt who were all captured and became POWs.

Further away from this area Messerschmitt Bf110 (3869) VJ+OQ flown from Augsberg by Rudolf **Hess**, deputy leader of the Nazi Party and close aide to Hitler, crashed at Floors Farm at **Bonnington Moor, Glasgow** on 10 May 1941. Hess landed by parachute at Eaglesham near Glasgow and hoped to contact the Duke of Hamilton in pursuance of a bizarre peace mission under taken without Hitlers' blessing. Hess was taken POW and after the war remained imprisoned in Spandeau jail Berlin until his death.

Thornaby Cemetery once again was the scene of an enemy burial, that of Oblt.E.Peirsert (pilot), Lt.Rudolf Bellof, Fw.Karl Kinder and Gefr.Gerhard Vogel who were recovered from their aircraft Ju88A-5(2227) M2+EK of2/Kfgp106 after flying into a cliff at Cliff Farm, **Staithes,** near Whitby at 12.06am on 10 July 1941 in bad weather.

During a daylight maritime enemy attack against shipping on 9 December 1941 at 10.50am, Hurricanes of **43** sdn shot down Ju88D-1 (1465) F6+CL, ten miles off Seaham with the loss of crew Lt.F.Bohme, Fw.W.Lentfert and Obfws.L.Volkfour and F.Schackert. On 16 January 1942 at 4.50pm ack-ack fire succeded in shooting down Ju88A-4(1612) S4+EH of 1/Kfgp506 which crashed into the sea. One of the crew Lt.D.Andresen was washed ashore in **Tynemouth Haven** on 27 January 1942 and is buried in **Hylton** cemetery, the three other members of the crew, Uffzs.F.Pett and J.Scholze and Fw.F.Gruschta remain missing.

During the Baedecker raids on York on 29 April 1942 Ju88D-1 (1334) M2+CH of 1/KFG106 piloted by Lt.Werner Boy was shot down and killed by W/O.Y.Mahe whilst attempting a forced landing at Tree Farm, **Elvington** near York. The remaining crew Uffzs.K.H.Kugler and N.Schnindler and Gefr.H.Muller who was injured were taken POW.

Just before Christmas 1942 the crew of Lancaster W4319 of **101** sdn based at Holme on Spalding Moor were interred in **Thornaby** cemetery. The Lancaster, diverted to Croft, was shot down on 17 December 1942 by not so friendly **South Gare** ack-ack fire, when returning from mining operations, and crashed near **Grangetown**. The crew of three New Zealanders Sgts.M.J.O'Malley, M.A.G.McIntyre and S.S.McLean, American Sgt.G.M.Georges of the RCAF and Sgt.George John Warren RAF(VR) were all killed. On that same night the crew of Obgefr.Gerhard Wight, Obgefr.Hans Rooschner and Obgefr.Franz Armann and Fw Wilhelm Stoll, found after a search lasting two days, were killed when their Dornier 217E-4 (4348) U5+AK of II/KG2 was shot down by ack-ack fire and crashed at **Ravenstones** on a remote site on Wheeldale Moor near **Goathland** at 10.00pm. They too are buried in **Thornaby** cemetery, a few paces from the Lancaster crew.

One mile east of **Chopgate** on Black Intake Moor on 12 February 1943 WellingtonIII BJ778 of RCAF **427 Lion** sdn from **Croft** crashed when returning from mine laying operations. All the crew were killed including P/O.Bryan Dunn and the pilot Sgt.Oscar Phillip Adlam who lie buried in **Thornaby cemetery** together with Sgt.Nav.Eric Sykes and F/O.Peter Ewart Davison, flying 2OTU Beaufighter R2152 from Catfoss, who were also fatalities in **Bilsdale** on 28 April 1943 when at 23.16 hours they were killed on **Urra Moor. Thornaby** cemetery is also the resting place of Canadian pilot F/L.Alan John Farquhar Symes (RCAF) who was killed at High Leven Farm near Sober Hall, **Leven** at 11.15am on 11 November 1943 whilst attempting a single engine landing in Mosquito DZ459 from 8OTU Dyce.

Many enemy aircraft as they returned home from raids on Britain. were shot down and crashed into the Sea off Britsh and **Dutch** coast by waiting RAF fighters. A similar ploy was used by the Luftwaffe off the **East coast of England** as allied planes returned home. Apart from incidents affecting Thornaby squadrons and enemy action over Teesside, hundreds of crashes in the near vicinity happened such as on 22 June 1941 at **Catterick Bridge** when Fortress AN522 of **90** sdn iced up at 33,000 feet, spun and lost a wing in the ensuing dive. Medical officer F/L.Steward survived. During 1941 two **55OTU** Hurricanes crashed, L1841 on 1 May at **Great Stainton** and W9261 on 14 September at **Elstob** near Sedgefield. On 18 December 1941 at Keanly Sides Farm, **Hurworth** Whitley V Z9308 of **78** sdn crash landed.

For some crashes rescue was near at hand. Two local Hartburn Village lads, dressed in best suits, who were returning home from a dance, recollect using a farm gate as a makeshift stretcher to rescue Canadian aircrew from Lancaster KB425 of **428** sdn which crash landed. Two crewmen were killed on 3 February 1945 just off Sandy Leas Lane. Six days earlier on 28 January another Canadian Lancaster KB763 of **419** sdn crashed and burnt out at Spring House farm. Only the rear gunner survived. Both incidents occurred near to the Gunnery HQ at **Elton Hall** on the outskirts of Stockton.

Wrecked aircraft, may have been just a badly bent aircraft but still intact, but more likely just a mass of twisted mass of alloy and steel strewn across the moorland, or even a hole in the ground. Wrecks were scattered all over the **North Yorkshire Moors**, although nowadays except in the most inaccessable areas it is most unlikely that even the minutest remnant of evidence remains as witness to wartime tragedies. Many squadrons endured the trauma of crashes happening so near to home base on the North Yorkshire moors. Some of which are mentioned here.

Wellington W5493 of 104 sdn (Driffield), ex operations Emden flew into a hill and exploded, on 10 January 1942 at **Arden Great Moor.**
Whitley V P4967 of 10 sdn (Leeming) after running out of fuel on return from 'operations' crashed on 4 September 1940 at **Nether Silton.**
Whitley V T4171 of 58 sdn (Linton) was shot up on 'operations' over Le Havre and crashed on 21 October 1940 at 6.00am at **Ingleby Greenhow.**
Lancaster I W4233 of 61 sdn (Syerston) after a raid on Kiel crashed killing two crewmen on 14 ctober 1942 at Haggs House Moor **Bilsdale.**
Lancaster ED481 of 9 sdn (Waddington) after being diverted to Leeming with engine failure after a raid on Hamburg crashed wuth the loss of seven lives on 30 January 1943 at Moor Gate near **Helmsley.**
Spitfire mkVb BL251 of 122 sdn (Scorton) lost control in cloud on 5 December 1941 and struck a hill at Mill Farm, Upsall, **Guisborough.**
Blenheim1F L1449 of 54 OTU (Church Fenton night fighter training school) on searchlight cooperation exercise crashed on 18 July 1941 at **Bransdale** Water Fall.
Spitfire crashed during February 1942 at **Rosedale** Abbey and pilot with both legs broken starved to death in snow.

When you take to the North Yorkshire Moors again, pause a moment to reflect on those wrecks scattered about the Moors and those who lost their lives in them.

There were prangs by the hundred, prangs by the score,
By the allies and the enemy, there were prangs galore,
In the valleys and the forests, and the North Yorkshire Moor
With so much beauty, yet for some a place of tragedy to endure.....by D.Webb

This Heinkel He111 was the FIRST German aircraft to be shot down on ENGLISH soil at Whitby...... 1940. The body of Uffz.J.Meyer lies in the snow with a machine gun nearby.

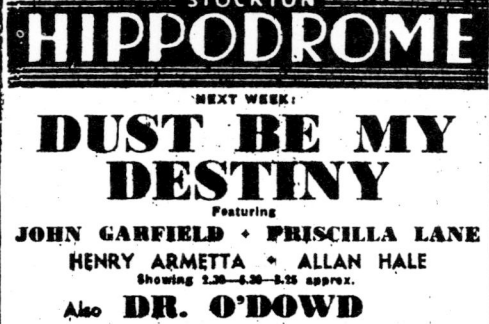

Entertainment! The film at the Hippodrome - STOCKTON reflects events of 15 August 1940

A Map showing events of 15 August 1940

**Air Battle of the North East
15 August 1940**

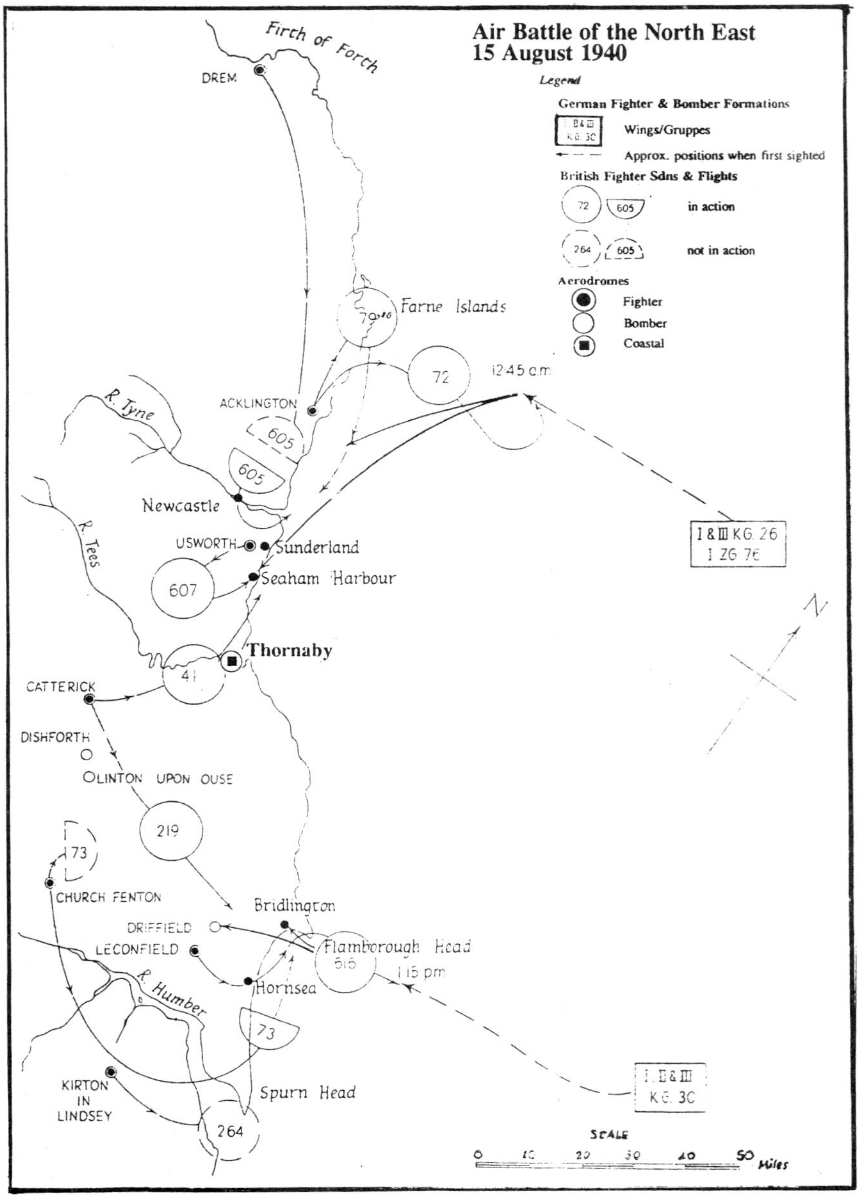

A DAY TO REMEMBER

The **Battle of Britain** started on 'Eagle Day'... 13 August 1940 and ended on 31 October 1940.... During the twenty four hours ending at midnight on 15 August 1940 the Luftwaffe made 1786 sorties...about 300 more than on Eagle Day. This was to be our 'Battle of Britain' which was popularly dubbed as the **'Battle of the North East'**. This was the first time that planned coordinated attacks in daylight by the three Luftlotten deployed from Norway to Brittany was put into effect, proving exceedingly expensive! Responsibility for the defence of this area rested with Air Vice Marshal Saul (Air) and Major Gen.Pargiter (Ack-ack). The area was attacked by 65 long range Heinkel IIIs from units I/KG26 and III/KG26 inadequately escorted by 35 Me110 twin engined fighters from I/ZG76 and defended by fighter aircraft from No.13 Grp backed by the guns of the 7th Ack-ack Division. Heavy casualties were inflicted and many enemy bombers were turned back well short of their intended airfield targets. Throughout the whole of the UK the Luftwaffe lost 75 aircraft against RAF losses of 34. In the area from the **Tyne to the Humber**, the enemy lost 16 bombers and eight fighters without loss to our own squadrons..... an achievement hailed by some as one of the great turning points of the Battle.

First plotted one hundred miles out to sea off the Firth of Forth and sighted at 12.30 hours the Luftwaffe were bound from Stavanger in Norway for targets in north east England, including the bomber airfields at Linton-on-Ouse and Dishforth. The honour of striking **FIRST** blow fell to the 11 Spitfires of **72 sdn** from **Acklington** some 30 miles from the coast at 22,000 feet. Though heavily outnumbered, **72 sdn** apparently took the enemy by surprise, some bombers jettisoned their bombs and took refuge in the clouds and the Me110s fighter escort, which seem to have been flying without rear gunners, concentrated on protecting themselves and leaving their charges to their own devices. 72 sdn claimed several hits on enemy planes without a single hit on their Spitfires.

Thereafter the German formation split into two...... one portion making for **Newcastle**, only to be attacked by the second Acklington squadron of Hurricanes of **79 sdn** which engaged the Me110s, which together with **605 sdn** Hurricanes from **Drem** and the **Tyne Ack-ack** guns, resulted in Heinkel11s dropping bombs which mostly fell in the sea away from the target...**RAF Usworth**. The southerly part of the force were severely buffeted by **41 sdn** from **Catterick**, **607 sdn** from **Usworth** and the **Tees ack-ack** guns and distributed their loads to little purpose, mostly near **Seaham Harbour** and Sunderland where some houses were destroyed. **Ouston** airfield was also strafed. One Hurricane from **605 sdn**, after battle with the enemy, ran out of fuel and force landed at Grayfields near **Hart** station, tippled on to its back and had to be removed by road. Enemy losses amounted to **eight bombers** and **eight fighters** during this encounter with local fighter squadrons.

At 2.00pm, 30 miles from **Middlesbrough** He111H-4 aircraft 1H+FS of 8/KG26 was shot down by fighters en route to attack Dishforth airfield and crashed into the sea. The crew of five, Lt.Renner, Fw.Baldauf, Obgefr.Roessiger, Gefr.Lorenz and Uffz.Schumann were all rescued unhurt and captured. Another He111-4 aircraft of 1KG/26 was shot down in the sea at Cresswell Bay off **Teesmouth** with all the crew of Flbr.Henrickenson Gefr.Machglitt Uffz.Zimmeran, Oblt.Koch and Gefr.Kulick captured. Other Heinkel HeIII H-4 crews of 8/KG26 also failed to return from their mission to attack Dishforth airfield following fighter attacks. They were Uffzs.Puschstein, Klug, Hofmann and Lotz and Lt.Burk; Oblt.von Lubke, Obfw.Hennicke and Uffz.Knauer who were killed and Uffz.Schlick who was missing; Oblt.von Besser and Uffzs.Brehm, Rohm, Hofmann and Reichert who were all missing; and Oblt.Riedel and three other NCOs who were also also missing. Five NCOs from one crew of 9/KG26 were killed and another crew of whom one NCO was killed and another wounded were picked up by a German Naval vessel after crashing in the **North Sea**. All the He111H-4 aircraft were lost.

Of the eight fighter losses one Messerschmitt Bf110D M8+CH of 1/ZG76 at 1.36pm was shot down by Spitfires from **72 sdn** at Steatham, near **Barnard Castle**. The crew of Oblt.Kettling and Obgefr.Volk were captured. A further five Bf110Ds and one Bf110C failed to return to their home bases. Gruppe Kommandeur Hptmn.Restemeyer and Hptmn.Hartwick of 1/ZG76 went missing off the east coast, near **Newcastle**, as did Gruppe Adjutant Oblt.Loobes and Uffz.Brock of 1/ZG76. One plane of 3ZG26 was lost off the north east coast in the **North Sea,** with the crew of Obfw.Groening and Obgefr.Hahn missing, believed shot down. Of the crew, from another plane M8+EK of 2/ZG76, Obgefr.Lenk was killed and Fw.Ladwein was rescued and survived as a POW. Two other planes one of which was a Bf110C of StabZG76 was last seen during combat and presumed shot down in the sea with loss of life to Oblt.Knap and Uffz.Neumayer. The other a Bf110D of 3/ZG76 was shot down off the **Northumberland** coast and the crew of Lt.Koehler and Uffz.Oelsner died. One other Bf110D fighter of 2/ZG76 which was severely damaged by fighters whilst escaping over the North Sea crash landed on return to Esberg with Uffz.Gershecker killed and Uffz.Richter wounded.

Meanwhile another action 90 miles south at 13.15 hours consisted of 50 unescorted Junkers 88s of mainly III/KG30 bound from **Aalborg** in Denmark for Yorkshire, targeted **Driffield** bomber airfield and were attacked by Spitfires, Defiants and Hurricanes from **73 sdn Church Fenton** of 12 Group, aided by Blenheims from **219 sdn** from **Catterick**. Nevertheless some 30 Ju88s reached **Driffield** and accurately bombed it and destroyed 12 **Whitley** bombers and four hangers and buildings. The Blenheims from Catterick helped chase the Ju88s for long distances overland and for a 100 miles or so out to sea. Fighter Command was without loss and as for the enemy, eight Ju88s bombers were shot down or crashed (one sdn losing half of their original nine aircraft) with one Ju88C (1/KG30) shot down near **Driffield** and another from 7/KG30 shot down at nearby **Hornby**. Local squadrons shot down a Ju88A of 4/KG30 at **Hunmanby** and another of 3/KG30 at **Bridlington** together with two Ju88Cs of III/KG30 both of which crashed, one off the **east coast** and another when attempting to land on return to **Aalburg** in Denmark. Two other Ju88Cs were either shot down (7/KG30) or were reported missing from combat (1/KG30). Two other planes on return from mission crashed on landing and were damaged, Ju88A-5 of II/KG30 at **Oldenburg** and Ju88c of IIIKG30 in **Holland.**

Elsewhere on that particular day throughout the UK honours were more even........but as for Thornaby and it's airfield and neighbours Stockton and Billingham and Greatham they escaped unscathed. It was indeed ....
A Day to Remember.

Part of a Spitfire from a crash site near Kirklevington. Pilot A.C.Deere survived to become an Air Commodore.

This German Me Bf110D fighter was shot down near Barnard Castle during the Battle of Britain

CAUSE FOR ALARM

The airfield had on it's doorstep much **heavy industry**. According to RAF observers it was adequately camouflaged, to prevent observation of specific and vulnerable targets and to make boundaries identification more difficult to detect from the air. Albeit the whereabouts of many factories were pin-pointed due to the shape of the **River Tees** and many were already known to the enemy to give `Cause for Alarm'. Hence the need for the defence activities of our aircraft, AA and balloons to harrass the enemy. The area was one of the **FIRST** industrial areas in the countries to be protected by barrage balloons. Every firm adapted or improvised to change from peace time to wartime production, to assist in airfield or aircraft construction, weapons or ammunition manufacture, building of naval (including fabrication in KD form for assembly by the quay side) or merchant vessels, to provide high octane fuel & hydrogen, shelters and be involved in **'D' Day** preparations.

Contributions made by some of the more famous well established firms are perhaps better known than some of their lesser known counterparts. Loss of skilled workers called up by HM Forces from factories, were replaced by women who had to handle many essential industrial tasks.

Much of our industry was dependent for survival on the iron and steel making industries of **Bells, Cargo Fleet, Cochranes, Dormans and Gjers and Mills.**

A poignant reminder that **aircraft** were being lost in battle by both the allies and the Luftwaffe was evidenced by the scarred remains of wings and fuselages of wrecked fighters and bombers as they were transported to the alloy metal reclamation plant along Durham Lane, Eaglescliffe at **Nuffields** No.2 Central Reclamation Depot (now the Royal Navy Stores Depot).

The value to the war effort, by industry on Tees-side, can be judged by the scarce nature of goods that were produced. Just one reason as to why the area attracted the attentions of the **Luftwaffe** and warranted such severe **defensive** measures.

Landmarks familiar to Luftwaffe planes and crews. The River Tees, Transporter Bridge and ICI factories.

Preston Hall at EAGLESCLIFFE. The wartime home of the Power-Gas Corpn & it's employees

The variety of ways in which companies responded to the needs of war can be seen at a glance at the below mentioned achievements.

Contributions made to the War Effort by Teesside Factories

Athol.G.Allan - makers of liquidified TNT which solidified in slabs for supply to the out lying ammunition factories at Newton Aycliffe.

Ashmores - mostly manufactured bombs, incendiaries and shell casings, Bailey bridges and railway bridge supports but mostly remembered for the huge fabricated caissons and floating bridges made jointly with Head Wrightsons for Mulberry Harbour but also constructor of a dozen hydrogen plants, hundreds of gas plants and a few dolomite (used to process magnesium) plants.

Cleveland Bridge - part of a consortium of companies formed to make Bellman unit construction hangers, also bridges for mulberry Harbour and fabricated KDs for Stockton Construction Co.

Davy & United - significant producers of case hardened steel used for the armour plating of gun casings, TCLs, corvettes, turbines, aircraft, bomb casings and 427 'complicated to make' tank turrets.

Dorman Long - fabricators of 'D' Day pier heads and floating docks and providers of 236 KDs and corrugated steel shelters at Bowesfield works.

Eaglescliffe Chemicals - producers of chrome oxide for use in chromium metals needed for jet engines and anhydrous sodium chromate for smoke screens.

Head Wrightson - manufactured bomb casings, four hundred Bellman airfield hangers and was involved with the fabrication of the PLUTO under sea oil line from the south coast to France at 'D' Day and making of KDs for Stockton Construction Co.

Hills - manufacturers of the all wood and plywood Hillson Praga monoplane since 1937 (at the Manchester) factory continued being involved with aeronautics throughout the war. The Stockton joinery shop converted to an aircraft factory, manufacturing aero ply for use on Mosquitoes, Ansons and Oxfords and making Jablo propellers (458,000 propellers were produced by six factories for use on Spitfires, Mosquitoes, Hurricanes and Lancasters). Hundreds of thousands of bundles of tin foil strips (window) were produced, in a Boathouse Lane factory, and were dropped on 'D' Day to confuse enemy radar. Uniquely styled Lamella roofed (to give more space in upstairs rooms) semi detached houses (as in Fairfield Road, Stockton) were also manufactured.

Hills (Richard) - manufacturer of steel track mesh for use on aircraft landing grounds.

Harkers - marine engines.

Imeson and Finch - specialised in manufacturing bombs parts (excepting fins, cases and explosive) for bombs varying from 250 to 4000lbs and was the first factory to make a 1000lb bomb container.

ICI - least known yet surely the most sinister activity was the Tube Alloys research project concerned with development of the **atom bomb**, and best known for the production of high octane fuel from creosote and victane from benzene and 'Pool' petrol from coal, nitric acid and ammonia nitrates used in explosives at Royal Ordnance Factories, ammonia used in case hardening, and methane used in RDX explosives and perspex. Famous for the PIAT gun (which featured in the awarding of six VCs), Rolls Royce engine parts, gun casings, keels and bailey bridges were also engineered.

Pickerings Lifts - manufacturer of lifts for ships, well remembered ammunition lifts for the cross channel guns on the south coast, Bailey bridges parts and pontoons, mulberry harbour, Tank wheels, anti-magnetic devices for use on mine detection vessels, aircraft hanger door lifting gear and barrage balloon winches.

Power Gas - constructors of hydrogen and bottle filling plants designed by ICI, and gas producer plants as back-up power for munition factories.

SD.I & S (The Malleable) - fabricator of KDs for Stockton Construction Co.

Stockton Construction Company - was a consortium of Cleveland Bridge, Head Wrightson, South Durham I.&.S and Whessoe which launched 243 KD vessels (made up of 218 LCTs, 17 gun boats and eight rocket/flak craft) at Richardson, Duck and Craig Taylor yards.

Tees Side Bridge & Engineering - constructors of airfield type T1 and T2 (T for temporary) hangers, nearest surviving example being at Teesside International Airport, indoor air raid shelters, auto and aero spares, and turrets for 'Churchill and 'Valentine' tanks and armoured cars. Dixons' yard was used to assemble and launch 292 KD vessels including 214 LCTs, 78 baby warships (30 floating gun platforms and 48 rocket platforms), some of which distinguished themselves at Walcheren in 1944, and ten salvage vessels.

Whessoe - storage tanks, munitions and KD kits for Stockton Construction Co.

Shipbuilders on Teesside built numerous tankers, trawlers and naval warships, barges, landing craft (LCs) and salvage vessels. **Furness'** yards built aircraft hangers in the early years, in addition to the launching through out the war of twenty six tankers (up to four hundred and eighty four feet length), two salvage vessels, one minelayer and ten cargo vessels and two naval sloops (HMSs Erne and Ibis) each armed with six 4 inch and 10 smaller guns. HMS Ibis was bombed by French aircraft in North Africa on 10 November 1942 which caused the deaths of Cdr.H.M.Darrell-Brown, 3 officers and 104 ratings. Sixteen ChanTs (channel tankers fabricated in sections by different firms) were assembled and launched and so were four LCTs for use on 'D' Day. Seven tankers were torpedoed or bombed and failed to survive the war of the Atlantic. **Smiths Dock** built 79 ships at their South Bank yard for WWII 26 of which were corvettes (mostly 'Flower Class' built during 1940/41), 20 frigates, five salvage vessels, two LSTs, six LCTs and 15 armed mine-sweeping trawlers. One tragic incident occurred on 24 May 1940 (the day when France surrendered) when the corvette HMS La Bastiaise was lost off Teesmouth together with 50 out of the 65 french crew and eight Smith Dock employees. A further four Flower class frigates were lost to U boat torpedoes during the Battle of the Atlantic, as were two trawlers in the English Channel and the frigate HMS Mourne was sunk by U boat torpedoes in the English Channel in operation 'Overlord'. **William Gray** - repaired 1,737 ships at the Graythorpe yard and built 74 colliers and bulk carriers and two piers for Mulberry harbour alongside the nine built at Normandy Wharf.

A Hillson Praga Monoplane. Once a world record holder. Built by Hills until early 1940.
Courtesy of Crosby Sarek Limited

One of many Tank Landing Craft built on Teesside. TCL 47 was launched from Cleveland Dock.

West Hartlepool (GREATHAM) Airport nearing completion. Bellman Hangers are in place. July 1938.   *Courtesy of the Hartlepool Mail*

THERE IF NEEDED - GREATHAM SATELLITE

Described by one senior government minister as the best grass aerodrome in the country. **Greatham** airfield was requisitioned by **RAF Thornaby** on 3 September 1939 as a Satellite.

The **FIRST** aerodrome in **Hartlepool** was sited in an area with Brenda Road to the south and Port Clarence Road to the east, and was used during World War One. Later during the 1930's Sir Alan Cobham and his flying circus used farm land which is now Owton Manor Lane. The second **aerodrome**, on land bought by the Corporation in 1935, was officially opened by the Secretary of State for Air, Sir Kingsley Wood on **15 April 1939**. Five acres of land was acquired by the RAF for use as a training centre in October 1937 and during mid 1938 the **32nd RAFVR FTS** was formed, as part of the Civil Air Guard, to teach young men to fly. Situated 3 miles from West Hartlepool Town centre and nine miles from Thornaby, Greatham airfield occupied 175 acres of land at the outbreak of WWII and was located east of and adjoined the village of Greatham, just two miles distant from the North Sea. Usual access was along a lane 24 feet wide, which passed through Greatham cottages, off the main A689 West Hartlepool to Stockton oad about one mile east from the village and a similar distance from Seaton Carew railway station The LNER Hartlepool - Stockton railway bordered on the south side.

On 3 Sept 1939 the RAFVR Flying Training school disbanded and left behind six Nissen huts and a bath house. Unauthorised access to the airfield was prevented by the use of triple loop barbed wire around the perimeter and road blocks were set up at Sappers Corner; midway between Sappers Corner and the airfield entrance; and at the bridge into the village on the old Stockton road. A **dummy air-strip** was created at Cowpen Cross. The AFS commandeered a Buick car which was coupled to a tender to form a mobile fire appliance, both of which were kept in the garage of a large house near the Green.

All building **work in progress** ceased except for the construction by Head Wrightson, of the third Bellman type hanger. The **hangers** barely had time to be used as they were all removed (possibly to Thornaby) some time during late 1939. During 1940 six wooden huts on the site were used by the RAF. One hut housed a link trainer and another was used as a cover for the emergency fire, ambulance and accident services provided by RAF Thornaby. Another hut doubled as a canteen and instruction room for pupil pilots. The crew room edged on to the services road. The only building of substance was made of wood with a brick annex for use by the chief instructor and pupils. Other huts were used for ground staff accommodation/stores/workshops and ammunition /fuel store. A machine gun range and gas depot was sited one hundred yards east of the main exit. The ex RAFVR Nissen huts, opposite the canteen, were acquired by army personnel and used as a barrack block. Two air raid shelters were erected on the main camp and the partially built Corporation owned club house was adapted to make a third shelter. Four perimeter **defence pill box** compounds were constructed to give a square like formation. Drainage was improved and the landing area increased by 43 acres to give an overall airfield size of 218 acres and a runway length of 1,400 yards. Red warning lights on Cerebos salt works and the 'mill' and landing lights were turned on as needed when airplanes were using the airfield. By early 1941 a crew room was also sited alongside the main service road and a small Nissen hut served as a guard hut at the Camp entrance.

Greatham was well **camouflaged** with a hedge of dead shrubs and tree branches signifying the extent of the usable part of the field. During May 1940 defences were alerted to the possibility of imminent invasion, when extra small arms and Bren guns were issued and two armoured cars were delivered. Each vehicle carried a set of four Vickers MGs which were operated manually using aircraft style sights. Detachments of army trained Ground Gunners (better known as the RAF Regiment from 1 February 1942 onwards) from **Thornaby** were responsible for the **airfield defence,** in association with the DLI (until 1942 when replaced by the Green Howards) who looked after the ground to ground anti-invasion defences of the airfield. The **RAF Regiment** later became responsible for all **airfield defence** functions. Entrances to pill box sites on the airfield and the main road entrance to HQ were guarded by Army personnel. Each pill box was manned by three GGs on guard duty two hours on then four hours off for three days then one day off. During the Winter of 1940 snow more than six feet deep, caused the GGs sited at Micklemire Lane, Red Barns and Greenhouses to be cut off from the rest of the camp, as a result of which they had to be supplied with weekly rations to enable them to cook their own meals. The GGs slept in tents at this time pending the construction of barrack huts. During early 1941 a hut for use by the GGs was also built next to the hut then used by the NAAFI sited near the Club House shelter. In the event of air raids all personnel except those on duty took to the shelters. Greatham was well fortified. Three pill boxes and A/T traps were sited to the west of the village alongside the Beck, a fourth near the cemetery, one to the south near Mickleton Lane..

Air raids occurred regularly. On 31 July 1940 the Prime Minister flew to Greatham on a moral boosting tour. Bombs were often dropped less than a 1,000 yards away from the landing field. On 26 August 1940 eleven HEs fell on Seaton Snooks. Bombs again fell on Catcote Farm on 18 September, rumour being that bombing was so habitual that they served as a night cap for the farmer. Then after a gap of six months on 13/14 March 1941 two para mines flattened Graythorpe. On 19 Aug 1941 seven HEs fell on Owton Grange Farm house and on 2 October 1941 Graythorpe was bombed again. Then during 1942 on 15/16 April four HEs fell on Owton Fens House. At 1.15am on 8 July 1942 at least eight HEs were dropped. The first fell in a field near the railway line about 1,000 yards south of the famous Hospital Chapel (founded in 1272). Three bombs fell on Cerebos Salt works, one of which failed to explode until 7.15am (just before workers arrived), completely gutting the canteen and box wood shop, severing brine lines and scattering glass and slates off the 'Bisto' and 'Saxa' premises over a wide area. Cerebos workers were certainly worth their salt as they stove to enable production to be resumed within two weeks. four other HEs fell around the brine wells. Several bombs including one UXB, two HEs at Throston Farm and eight 'Firepots' at Tunstall Manor Garden dropped on 14 December 1942 causing no casualties. The last raid in the area was on 22 July 1943 when bombs were dropped on Seaton Snooks.

Ack-ack gun positions were established in the area to deter enemy attackers, located at Pudding Nook (now Phillips petrol farm), Sappers corner, the Co-op Farm and behind the Black Swan in Cowpen, supplemented by mobile units at Ceribos salt works. A **searchlight unit** was set up at West Meadow farm. Ack-ack positions were also established off the Hart side of Easington Road near the General Hospital. Later, on the Town Moor one hundred and four 'Z' Rocket projectiles were installed.......never used in anger so it is said.

Greatham was used a **satellite** base for **Thornaby** and as a forward fighter base by **fighters** attached from **Catterick**, for convoy duties whenever convoys were moving in the area. As there were no permanent aircraft servicing facilities at this 'primitive' airfield, in the event of fighters being scrambled they had to return to their own base for refuelling. **Spitfires** from sdns 41 and then 54 from RAF **Catterick** via Thornaby were attached to Greatham at times varying from a few minutes to a few hours or all day, right from the opening of hostilities until 28 July 1941 in a 'state of readiness'. Bad weather conditions often necessitating crews leaving aircraft at Greatham whilst meals and overnight billet were sought at Thornaby. On 3 April 1940 a Spitfire of 41 sdn entered the **history** books when it became the **FIRST** fighter aircraft to be shot down by the **Luftwaffe** whilst defending Great Britain during WWll. Flown by F/L Norman Ryder, a Spitfire left Greatham (on detachment from Catterick) to intercept a Heinkel lll Bomber which was harassing shipping. During combat adversaries shot each other down, both crews being rescued from their ditched aircraft by trawler men. Accidents were frequent. Three Beaufighters of 41 sdn crashed within days of each other around this time when landing

During the Battle of Britain Greatham and Thornaby were both witness to a **'A Day to Remember'** during a lunchtime raid on 15 August 1940.

As a result of this attack one flight from 54 sdn were kept at 'Readiness' at Greatham and spent mostly very boring days with only a telephone for company which very rarely rang! Later in September 1940 one section did flying training whilst the other remained 'Ready'. Perhaps one Polish Spitfire pilot of 54 sdn was a little too ready, disappearing in pursuit of a Ju88 sighted near Whitby, never to be seen again.

Starting January 1942, **6(C)OTU** used Greatham for their

training, practicing circuits and bumps (landings and take offs) and gunnery practice until March 1943. N Flight Anti-AA co-op unit (redesignated **1613 flight** on 1 October 1942), moved from **Thornaby** on 4 May 1942, using a Tiger Moth and four Henleys, and left during February 1943 for Hutton Cranswick to be absorbed in 291 sdn. During this period Spitfires from the newly formed **332 Norwegian sdn**, from 16 January 1942 until 9 June 1942 (whilst preparing for operations over France), and then a replacement detachment of four Spitfire Vs from **RCAF 403 sdn** (whilst resting at Catterick after operations over France) from 19 June 1942 to 22 January 1943, were used at Greatham. Throughout 1942 these Spitfires gave cover to **6(C)OTU** whilst training at Thornaby. Prangs were minimal and usually without severe damage involving Spitfires, Hurricanes, Ansons and Hudsons although it has been suggested that a Lancaster made a force landing on one occasion. Owing to its location this airstrip, aligned SW/NE, was never developed and ceased to be used as a **satellite airfield** in Mar 1943.

Many **off duty hours** were spent in Smiths Arms, the Bull and Dog and the Hope and Anchor better Known as top, middle and bottom houses, all of which were owned by The Hospital at Greatham. But the main attraction was at old Hartlepool which boasted a public house on every street corner. Cinema goers were well catered for by the 'Northers' and 'Regal' in York Road, the 'Electric', the 'Queens' and the 'Picture House' in Stockton Road together with live cabaret and vaudeville at the 'Empire'. In the chapel school room the WI provided tea, books to read and a piano to play and the Church Institute offered a game of billiards and a monthly dance. Serviceman were always made to feel at home in both Greatham and Hartlepool.

During 1943, coinciding with the cessation of **6(C)OTU** at Thornaby the airfield was completely reorganised. The existing buildings were put to different uses. The chief instructors hut became the watch office and the old crew room became the WT centre. A new brick and asbestos building erected near the compass platform was used as a Flight Office and Rest room. New MT, Petrol, oil and fuel compounds were built on the site of a Bellman hanger and a static water tank built on the corporation hanger site. The Guard hut on entry to the airfield was replaced by a Guard House. Substantial bomb storage and handling facilities were constructed in the south east corner of the airfield near the small pond and on the west side the bulk petrol installation was upgraded to 24,000 gallon capacity. This concentrated activity continued for a few weeks. To **accommodate** the anticipated extra numbers of personnel, camp sites were established off the airfield (one near the cemetery which is now a Primary School, another east of the Green - now Queensway and a third at Fence House Farm one hundred yards north of Sappers corner and a fourth at Sappers corner which also housed the messing facilities which were capable of feeding 707 persons (42 officers, 125 sergeants and 540 other ranks). The messing site included messes, dining rooms, Institute, medical inspection and accident room, and the luxury of a bath house, effectively converting Greatham into a self contained station. **Accommodation** consisted of four officers huts, 12 sergeants huts and 15 other ranks huts spread more or less equally over four camp sites. 11 air raid shelters to cope with 50 men each, were built on the camp sites and eight blast shelters were erected on the messing site.

After **D Day** there was an exodus of airmen, which were replaced by military units of the 4th 'Holding' battalion, which reformed then returned to active duty. At December 1944 it seems that 36 Officers, 182 NCOs and 446 other ranks were still based at Greatham!

Shortly after **cessation of hostilities,** most of the thirty or forty temporary Nissen and wooden huts and eight brick buildings clustered around the still part built corporation Club House and bulk petrol installation were purchased from the Air Ministry by the **West Hartlepool Corporation**. Eventually all flying activities officially ceased during 1956 when the airfield was sold to **British Steel Corporation** for use as a steel works, during the construction of which at least one aircraft attempted a landing. So like many other wartime airfields Grantham ceased to exist........ with only the ghost of a Polish pilot clad in flying gear reputed to roam around the Steelworks' offices.

ACCIDENTS AND OPERATIONS

Operations covered tracts of the North Sea stretching from Montrose to Flamborough and reaching out to Norway and the Lowland countries. The priciple aim being to protect allied convoys and to impede enemy shipping movements. Operations resulted in many tragedies and accidents to both allied and enemy aircraft and crews.

During the three years until early 1942 that 608 and 220 sdns operated from Thornaby over the North Sea, Coastal Command sdns sunk 107 enemy ships during anti-shipping operations for the loss of 648 aircraft at an average of 239 tons of shipping per plane lost, and 369 ships sunk during mining operations for 329 aircraft lost at an average of 980 tons per plane l ost. To fly from Thornaby was no less difficult a matter of survival than for air crews of Fighter and Bomber Cmds.

Immediately prior to the outbreak of war air crews based at Thornaby used the **Seal Sands** Gunnery Range at the mouth of the River Tees for practice firing. Soon after the declaration of war on 3 September 1939, as individuals began to wake up to the realities of war many requests were made to RAF Thornaby to photograph camouflaged buildings and factories. ICI Billingham claimed to be the first factory to have it's camouflage photographed from the air using **colour film**. Time was spent addressing complaints about well known landmarks being silhouetted on the skyline and checking camouflage of military establishments in the area. Flying cooperation flights were made with the Army based at Catterick and elsewhere.

The pilots of 224 and 608 sdns were sometimes used, to ferry pilots based at Catterick to collect Spitfires from Shawbury, or to collect Ansons from Cosford and Hudsons from Shawbury. But the real tasks of **608** sdn were to locate surface mines which were subsequently destroyed by mine-sweepers of the Royal Navy, the sighting of U Boats or ships suspected of aiding the enemy and searching for small boats carrying refugees and escapees in addition to guarding North Sea convoys. This searching of vast expanses of sea, often without reward, was nicknamed the 'kipper patrol'. A similar role was carried out by Hudsons of **220** sdn in addition to reconnaissance duties. The **FIRST** operational patrol by a 220 sdn Hudson involved searching for a Belgian mv suspected of refuelling U Boats. Their **FIRST** action took place on 13 September 1939 when an Anson used anti submarine 100lbs bombs to attack a surfaced U Boat which submerged and apparently escaped. The **FIRST** operational flight by **608** sdn on 21 September 1939 was by Anson N5207 flown by S/L.G.Shaw with F/O.Woolcock, WOp.LAC.Kelly and Cpl.Knott as crew, on an anti submarine patrol, in response to a false alarm. During four combats with German flying boats during September 1939 **224** sdn lost one Hudson crew and suffered further loss on 7 October 1939 when three Hudsons shot down a Do18

The first flying mishaps of the war were caused, not by the enemy but due to collisions on the ground, overshooting the runway on landing, direction finding problems, stalling on take off, and under carriage failures. Early losses included **Anson** K6202 of **220** sdn which overshot the runway and crashed through a hedge on 25 September 1939. **Anson** K6152 crashed in similar circumstances at Catterick on 13 October 1939 and **Anson** K8825 of **220** sdn collided with another **Anson** of **608** sdn. Then more seriously **Anson** N5204 was shot down by a **Hurricane** from Digby over the North Sea near **Humber Lighthouse** on **27 October 1939**. Crew members F/L.Garnett, Actg.P/O.Baird and Cpl.Wilson perished and AC.Smith was wounded. The latter two were picked up by HMS Ganges. The funeral of Cpl.Wilson took place in St.Cuthberts R.C Church, Stockton. Next day an **Anson** and a **He111** were both attacked and shot down by a **Spitfire** of **602** sdn east of **May Island**.

Accidents were caused due to lack of fuel, lack of recognition by our own aircraft and AA especially when returning to base during air raids, apart from aircraft malfunction or pilot error. Accidents occurred frequently. A serious one was when **Hudson** N7290 of **220** sdn stalled on approaching landing and crashed on a house at 65, Cambridge Road, **Middlesbrough** on 8 November 1939. The crew of P/O.Ryan and Sgt.R.Mitchell (pilots), AC1.Wade and New Zealander P/O.D.H.Robertson (passenger) from **608** sdn were all killed. A few days later **Hudson** N7284 and crew from **220** sdn was lost whilst taking part in an air firing exercise.It crashed in the sea 4 miles east of **Seaham** with the loss of P/O.Hubert John Keller (RNZAF) and pilot

P/O.John White Crickton Robertson who was released from duty that day in order to gain more flying experience.

The **FIRST** ever attack by Coastal Command on the enemy at sea, was made on 13 December 1939, when a **Hudson** of **220** sdn attacked two enemy destroyers in the North Sea. Days later on 27 December 1939 a **Hudson** of **220** sdn shot down Do18D float plane 8L+CK of 2/Kfgp906 over the North Sea.

Interference, thought to emanate from ICI Billingham, overhead telephone lines or suspect enemy radio beacon transmissions often affected **communications.** Two pigeons were carried by each aircraft of Coastal Command. In emergencies, pigeons with messages attached were thrown out of the bomb bay of the aircraft in distress and with luck returned home. The message was conveyed to RAF Thornaby by telephone and dispatch rider. On 2 February 1940 **Anson M** N5199 of **608** sdn ditched in the sea six miles off **Blyth** and stayed afloat for forty five minutes. One pigeon escaped with a message as a result of which the crew were rescued. On 2 April 1943 a Hudson aircraft was reported to be in distress off the Scottish coast via a message carried by pigeon which arrived at Redcar after covering 150 miles in 6 hours.

On 3 February 1940 **Anson E** of **608** sdn, whilst escorting convoy FS85, spotted and attacked three **He111Ks** and forced them to turn tail. An emergency air attack warning was signalled to 19 Fighter Group which resulted in aircraft from 43 sdn **Acklington** attacking the invaders, one of which was destroyed and another damaged 15 miles east of **Tynemouth**. This contrasted to an incident the previous month on 19 January 1940, following an attack by a **Me110**, when the navigator reportedly had a pencil shot out of his hand, yet lived to tell the tale. Tthe **Hudson** limped home after inflicting damage on his adversary. At **Great Ayton** on 11 February 1940 **Hudson** N7294 of **220** sdn shortly after take off demolished a stone wall and crashed 300 yards west of Captain Cooks Monument. The belly was ripped out of the aircraft but AG.Sgt.Barker, who injured nought but two toes, survived and staggered, with only one shoe on to a nearby farm house. A Pigeon, trained by Mr.Hartas of Grove Hill, though injured, survived the crash at 4.15am and returned home and later received an award in recognition of bravery. Crew member F/O.T.M.Parker (pilot) lies buried in **Thornaby cemetery.**

The enthusiasm of the local squadrons, especially **608** sdn, coupled with their local knowledge and the fact that they were involved in protecting their own part of the world helped to make their contribution to the war effort more meaningful.

Probably the most famous incident in the wartime history of RAF Thornaby relates to the hunt for the **'Altmark'**, which was the auxiliary German supply 'prison' ship of the pocket battle ship Graf Spee. The 'Altmark' was located near Norway on 16 February 1940 by **Hudson K** of **220** sdn which took off from Thornaby together with other Hudsons of 220 sdn to search for the 'Altmark' finding her at 12.55 hours. The 'Altmark' was shadowed until interception, by **HMS Cossack** of the Royal Navy in Norwegian waters on the orders of Winston Churchill. The 'Altmark' was boarded by men of the Royal Navy and 299 allied merchant navy POWs were released on 16 February 1940. **Hudsons** from **224** sdn then took over from **220** sdn to escort the destroyer, with POWs on board, to a place of safety.

April 1940 saw the advent of the **Norwegian invasion** which called for extensive work by **608** and **220** sdns involving photographic reconnaissance and close escort duties to troopships and warships. **608** sdn did 131 patrols during April. Detachments of **224** sdn operating from Thornaby photo reconnaissanced **Wilhelmshaven, Sylt and Heligoland**. Frequent searches made for ditched aircraft often resulted in dinghies being located minus occupants. **Hudson** N7289 and N7283 of **220** sdn were shot down over **North Sea** on 24 April 1940. On 30 March **Hudson** N7237 of **220** sdn crashed after take off.. another write off. Whilst Hudsons were flying to Norway and North Germany, the enemy flew aircraft along the same paths in the opposite direction, which resulted in many an air to air encounter. Hudsons took on the roll of fighter bombers with the second pilot acting as a navigator/bomb aimer. In May 1940, **220** sdn were notably engaged as fighters in the evacuation of troops and protection of troop convoy from **Norway.** Then in **'Operation Dynamo'** at Dunkirk until 4 June 1940 they provided airborne cover for the safe evacuation of 338,226 allied troops when it was claimed that of 40 Ju87s attacked five were shot down. A **Do18** of 1/Kfgp406 was forced down in the **North Sea** on 10 May 1940 by three

Hudsons of **220** sdn and was subsequently sunk by a destroyer who rescued the crew of four, one of whom was dead and three others became POWs. On 13 May 1940 **Anson R3316** escorted **HMS Kelly**, with Captain Mountbatten (better known as **HRH The Duke of Edinburgh**) aboard to the Tyne after it had fought E Boats off Heligoland and suffered 27 fatalities.

During June. On 3 June **Hudsons** of **220** sdn raided oil tanks at **Rotterdam**. Two more fatal incidents occurred. On 11 June 1940 pilots WOp.AC1.W.C.Irving, AG.Sgt.J.C.Butterworth, and Sgts.D.R.Holbecke and E.Morgan were killed, when **220** sdn **Hudson P5127** crashed one mile away from Thornaby airfield at **Quarry Farm** and lie buried in **Thornaby cemetery**. On 19 June **Anson N5067** of **608** sdn crashed after take off and hit HT cables 4 miles from **Guisborough**. Sgt.Walpole died in North Ormsby hospital.

Hudsons of **220** sdn sunka 6,000 tons ship off Kirstiansund, Norway on 22 June 1940. During July ex WWI HMS Titania submarine depot ship was escorted to safety. On the 2nd **Hudsons** of **220** sdn attacked **Aalborg** and on 16 July onwards aircraft of coastal command carried out round the clock anti-invasion patrols over the North Sea. The Thornaby squadrons patrolled as far east as the **Frisians** from dawn until dusk with cover from **Bircham Newton** squadrons during the day. Hudsons and Ansons were each capable of carrying ten 100lbs or four 250lb bombs. **Ansons** were less aggressively armed than Hudsons. At best armament was four machine guns (including one fixed Browning operated by the pilot) compared to a Hudsons proble four .303s plus two fixed Brownings operated by the pilot and two .303s in turret yet had to be to be prepared to fight off the attentions of more powerful adversaries like Ju88s and He111s. The **Norway** and **Danish** coasts were patrolled by **Hudsons** to locate possible invasion fleets, to seek and then strike against enemy shipping and to protect allied convoys against 'hit and run' tactics of the enemy. In the event of a major confrontation the enemy would be distracted whilst warning was passed to standby fighter aircraft. **Hudson N7231** of **220** sdn collided with a barrage balloon cable and crashed at **Bolden Colliery** on 11 July 1940. Due to an unlit runway at Catterick on 2 August, **Hudson N7314** piloted by F/L.Harold Wentworth Aylward Sheahan DFC (credited with shooting down three enemy aircraft) of **220 sdn**, had to divert due to enemy aircraft being in the area, via Maltby to Thornaby, in fog. Unfortunately the aircraft hit overhead cables and crashed at **Thornton Grange Farm**. The bombs exploded and killed three of the four crew including the pilot, the second pilot P/O.Charles James Allsup and WOp.Sgt.Sydney Smith. Sheahan and Smith are buried in **Thornaby cemetery**. The rear gunner Sgt.Eric Bale Butler escaped with minor injuries. At this time other Hudsons were distrusted due to reports that one was being used by the Luftwaffe which could well be true.

During the **Battle of Britain** Thornaby was witness to a lunchtime raid on 15 August 1940 when (according to one newspaper report in 1941) 36 out of 40 enemy aircraft were shot down by fighter aircraft based at **Acklington, Usworth and Catterick**, with no losses sustained by our own North East attackers. The day after that epic battle on 16 August **Hudson N7316** of **220** sdn crashed after take-off at **Thornaby** and as the **Battle of Britain** reached a climax on 15 September yet another Hudson, **N7233** of **220** sdn crashed on takeoff.

The dreaded **Botha** was the cause for many anxious moments amongst crews of **608** sdn. On 24 August 1940 **Botha L6209** crashed at **Ormesby** after take off. Two crew were injured. A week later on 1 September 1940 **Botha L6165** on night flying training, piloted by P/O.Terence Hugh Creed, with ground crew AC1 Thomas Edward Corrigan and AC2 George Beadnell as passengers was warned away from the airfield due to a 'Red Alert' and were never seen again. Not a single a Botha aircraft was involved in combat whilst at Thornaby. **Swordfish** aircraft carried out mine-laying and bombing operations from **Thornaby** around coastal areas of the low countries.

Out of sheer frustration unofficial gun practice was occasionally carried out. One incident involved shooting up Goosepool Airfield at zero feet much to the discomfort of the contractors there. The aggressive fighting and protective spirit of Thornaby based Hudsons was well demonstrated when **Hudson T7310** of **220** sdn attacked a Heinkel on 25 September 1940. On 10 November **Do18D(0804) K6+DL** of 3/Kfgp406 was shot down by two **Hudsons** of **220** sdn and sank in the sea north east of **Scarborough**. The crew, apart from Oblt zur see Lutjens who was missing, were rescued by a

Dutch ship. The **FIRST** enemy aircraft sighted by **608** sdn was by the crew of P/O.Gibbs, F/L.Johnson, Sgt.Norton, and AG.Sgt.Gowing on patrol in **Anson** L R9577 on 11 November 1940. They were the first of many **608** sdn to engage in aerial combat, and claimed a **He115** float plane and possibly damaged another. Visibility was 12 miles and cloud at 1,800 feet when two He115s made a head on diving attack and opened cannon fire at 800 yards. Both He115s received hits and one gun was silenced. By skilful evasive action their own aircraft avoided being damaged. On 15 November 1940 S/L.Hodgkinson in a **Hudson** of **220** sdn, whilst searching the North Sea around **Skaggerak**, shot down a Heinkel float plane. Next month on 4 December 1940 **Hudson** P5135 of **220** sdn crashed in the sea off **Hartlepool**. Quite often practice 'dog fights' viewed from Thornaby in the skies above were not always accident free. One such incident culminated in a mid air collision at 12,000 feet on 28 December 1940 at Catterick whilst trainee Spitfire pilot Sgt.Squires underwent final stringent passing out tests with flight commander A.C.Deere of 54 sdn (a celebrated Battle of Britain pilot and later Air Commodore). Both pilots baled out and survived. Sgt.Squires landed at Kirkleatham Hall and his Spitfire crashed on the banks of the **River Leven** at Red Hall Farm. A.C.Deere landed in a cess-pit at Town End Farm in **Kirkleavington** and his Spitfire crashed nearby. Sgt.Squires was shot down on his first operational mission, crash landed and was taken POW. About this time night flying intensified and so did encounters with Heinkels and Dornier 215s. More accidents.. **Hudson** N7298 of **224** sdn detached fromLeuchas to Thornaby on 11 January 1941 crashed at **Kildale** and the crew died from injuries sustained when the aircraft broke up on impact. They clambered clear of the wreckage in appalling weather conditions with freezing fog and several feet of snow. A few days later the wreckage was spotted near Park Nab on Warren Moor just one mile from the village of Kildale. All the crew of Sgt.Keith Barnet Files, P/O.Basil Lincoln Fox, AG.P/O.John McDonald Scott Wylie and WOp/AG.Sgt.William Robert Martin died from exposure. The latter two named crew men lie buried in **Thornaby cemetery**. On 16 January 1941 **Hudson** P5151 of **220** sdn mysteriously crashed into the sea at about 11.00am NE of **Redcar**. Pilot P/O.Bryan John Ralph George, navigator Sgt.Albert Alan Cross and WOp/AG.Sgts.Jack Chester and Francis Hughes were killed. Days later on 22 January **Hudson** T9317 piloted by Sgt.Scase with WOp/AG.Sgt.W.Parritt as crew were both killed when their aircraft crashed at Scarth Nick near **Osmotherly** en route to St.Eval. One survivor raised the alarm at **Osmotherly**. On 24 February **Hudson** P5158 of **220** sdn attacked a Do215. On 11 March a **Hudson** of **220** sdn shot down a HE59 off Esberg and the **Hudson** piloted by Jack Hall shot down a Do215. Two **Ansons** of **608** sdn were lost when R9818 ditched and R9817 crashed in the sea on the 7 March. Whilst on a mission on 19 April 1941 WOp/AG.Sgt.Symes, was killed in a **BlenheimIV** of **114** sdn and is buried in **Thornaby cemetery**.

Cooperation between the Royal Navy and Coastal Command often paid handsome dividends. On 21 May 1941 aerial reconnaissance confirmed that the 'Bismark' and 'Prinz Eugen' ships had left the safety of a Fjord in Bergen, Norway. Next day in atrocious weather with low cloud and gale force winds every available coastal command aircraft patrolled the Norwegian coast. On 23 May HMS Suffolk sighted and shadowed their quarries. During the Battle on the 24th shell fire from `Bismarck' and `Prinz Eugen' sunk HMS Hood. Attacks by Fulmers and Swordfish aircraft from HMS Victorious caused negligible damage so under cover of bad weather 'Bismarck' and 'Prince Eugen' escaped and evaded aerial reconnaissance until 26 May. 'Bismark' was again sighted by a Catalina and attacked by Swordfish from the carrier HMS Ark Royal off the south west coast of England With her steering gear damaged and speed reduced to ten knots **'Bismark'** was crippled by torpedoes and gunfire from five destroyers and was finally torpedoed by cruisers Devonshire and Norfolk and scuttled by Admiral Lutjens on May 27 1941. **'Prinz Eugens'** escaped from this encounter. A year later on 17 June 1942 when bound for Keil, she was sighted by P/O.J.B.Austin in an (ex Thornaby) **608 sdn Hudson** based at **Wick**. The major strike force of 54 aircraft sent to attack lost nine planes during air combat with 20 Me109s. A memorable episode in the history of 608 sdn.

On 10 September 1941 **Hudson** AM561 from **608** sdn, whilst under going air tests over Tees mouth was attacked.

The guns were not loaded and the intercom was unplugged. Only skilful evasive sea level tactics by pilot P/O.J.Berry (later killed during raid on Norway on 2 November 1941) and eventual prolonged firing from belly gunner WOp/AG.Sgt.J.Chambers forced the Ju88 to quit the encounter. The damaged Hudson landed safely with an injured navigator.

During the last quarter of 1941 Hudsons from **608** and **220** sdns searched Norway fjords for enemy targets, attacked the ports of Esberg and Aalberg in Denmark, destroyed aircraft and runways and harassed enemy shipping off the Dutch coast and dropped **propaganda leaflets**, code named 'Nickel', throughout the low countries. One Ju88 was shot down in combat over Bergen in Norway during one such mission. During another raid, **Hudson** AM688 piloted by P/O.Lane sunk a German troopship which was docked at Esjberg. The Hudson was diverted to **Acklington** due to bad weather at Thornaby. During **608** sdn's **FIRST** night raid, led by Peter Vaux two ships were sank at **Esjberg** during October 1941. Other missions involved night photography of enemy installations in Norway. **Hudsons** of **608 sdn** at **Thornaby** lost AM599 on 2 September off **Norway, AM657** and **AM642** off the Frisians Islands on 5 November, **AM883** near **Aberdeen** on 16 November and **AM715** on 23 November whilst on patrol. On 30 December 1941 **Hudson** AM880 of **608** sdn wa DBRThese operations resulted in severe losses, in one three week period alone ten Hudsons were lost, one of which was piloted by CO of **608** sdn W/C.R.S.Darbyshire who was killed off Norway on 2 November 1941. Anti-shipping attacks along the coast of Norway were some of the most dangerous of all RAF flying activities, which involved low level bombing attacks. The aim of these attacks was to interupt the iron ore trade between Sweden and Germany and supplies to occupied Norway. The **'Gold Run'** convoys were heavily defended by flak ships and fighters and offered air crews only a one in five chance of survival on each tour undertaken.

The importance of training could never be over emphasised and air crews were always alerted for likely German reconnaissance flights patrolling the North Coast. On average ten aircraft per day were written off due to flying accidents every day throughout the war. Usually a Hudson trainnee crew comprised a Pilot, navigator and two WOps/AGs and after a course at an OTU were posted as a crew to their first operational squadron. **Training with OTUs** included both night and day exercises in navigation, bombing and gunnery in an area 20 miles out to sea from **Redcar**. One pilot's log typically reported circuits and landing, trips to Hartlepool, formation flying, air to air firing, all of which involved 106 flying hours during 12 weeks training. Each pilot learnt a 'Bad weather Approach' to Thornaby which could be rather tricky with the terrible smoke haze which enveloped the Tees estuary and the ever present balloon barrage, Each pilot worked out his own approach using familiar landmarks. Often fumes from ICI proved a useful aid to navigation. Pilots, apart from learning to fly a Hudson and spent 20 hours in a link trainer and were instructed on vital Hudson systems such as hydraulics, deicing procedures, flaps, gun turret operations, auto pilot, radar, signals and codes and dinghy and parachute drill. Night flying was practiced during daylight by simulating darkness. The student pilot wore special goggles through which could be seen the sodium lit flare path and instrument panels and was monitored by an instructor. The flying skill or lack of it was obvious with some pilots having no feel for engines or unable to judge distance. One pilot it was said attempted to land Hudsons either fifty feet above or below the ground. Once flying solo the pilot acquired a crew and gained experience in air navigation dead reckoning without radio, formation flying and night flying navigation. Crashes were quite regular events. Probably the **FIRST Hudson** lost with **6(C)OTU** was on 24 August 1941 when T9348 swung on take off and was destroyed. Then T9405 stalled and crashed near Newham Hall in **Nunthorpe** on 14 October 1941 and killed F/O.Wm.H.Dimmock who lies buried in **Thornaby cemetery** where Australian Sgts.Ronald.A.Glass and Colin.G.Quick also rest due to **T7228** which stalled on approach and caused their deaths on 6 November 1941. A ball of fire was seen to fall out of the sky over Eaglescliffe by newly arrived No.5 intake of 6(C)OTU on 18 December 1941 when the worst ever accident at **Thornaby** occurred when **Hudson** V9032 of 6(C)OTU stalled on take off and crashed on Quarry farm at **Ingleby Barwick**. Three airmen, F/Sgt.Graves (pilot), P/O.van Heerdan (observer) and WOp/AG.Hogg were killed midst the inferno and lie buried in **Thornaby cemetery**. Two children in the farm house miraculously escaped but Ray Garbutt, his wife and their two other children were killed.

Near the end of 1941 a **Hudson** crew whilst returning to Thornaby during an exercise radioed that the elevator controls had jammed and abandoned their aircraft as they crossed the coast. All the crew baled out to safety, uninjured. Just before Xmas **Hudson** N7243, piloted by Sgt.Dunnett of **6(C)OTU**, experienced the same problem and crash-landed on farm land near **Middlesbrough**. None of the crew suffered severe injury. Many prangs were caused due to the pilot selecting the wrong lever for undercarriage, flaps and bomb doors which were grouped closely together on Hudsons. One 6(C)OTU pilot belly flopped with bomb doors open at Goosepool. Canadian (later G/C) E.L.Bardoux whilst trying to land in the fog landed minus under carriage ative during early 1942. On another occasion the same pilot landed a **Hudson** in fog amongst a mine field on **Seaton** sands. After telephoning RAF Thornaby requesting fuel and new propellers he was able to make the shortest take off ever before the tide came in. Mishaps continued. **Hudsons** T9368 overshot and crashed on landing on 13 March 1942. **T9395** and **AM872** crashed on 25 March 1942. Many accidents due to heavy landings caused under carriage failure and loosened rivets which secured fuel tanks in place with risk of fuel leakage and poteneial fire. As Luftwaffe air power started to wane so did air crews in the final stages of training crews take part more often in real missions. Some of whom were destined never to see home base again. The entry in the War Register simply stated death **'Due to War Operations'**, like F/O.Hy.Kelso Dryden of the RAAF who lost his life on 27 March 1942, and lies buried in **Thornaby cemetery** when **Hudson** AM847 crashed. For the greater number of **6(C)OTU** fatalities the fateful entry stated death **'due to flying accident'** as on 17 April 1942 when **Hudson** T9378 hit a tree at Manfield Farm, **Thornaby**. Sgt.Cliff McCormick Carkner(RCAF) was killed and buried at **Thornaby cemetery**.

A typical **6(C)OTU** intake was made up of 20 pilots (9 RCAF Offrs., 7 RCAF Sgts., 1 SAAF Offr., 1 RAF Offr.& 2 Sgts.), 20 RCAF Sgt.Observers & 40 WOp/AGs (30 RAF Sgts., 2 RAF Offrs., 4 RCAF Sgts. & 4 RAAF Sgts.), many of whom had previously logged as few as 30 flying hours in De Haviland Rapides at Yatesbury P/O.Gibson Ritchie Stratford RCAF was captain of the only crew missing from that intake of 80 men, which stayed at Thornaby from 21 April 1942 until 14 July 1942. When on exercise with 6(C)OTU over the North Sea to Norway on 31 May 1942 the crew of **Hudson** T9279, WOp/AG.Sgt.Arthur Francis Gregory (buried at **Trondheim**). Ob.Sgt.Edwin Albert Young (buried at **Spangereid**), Wop/AG.Sgt.Dennis Roy Laddams and the Captain all failed to return. Accidents curtailed completion of this course. During practice landings one Hudson was wrecked and a RAF Regiment barrack hut, which was empty at the time, was demolished. Fuel starvation caused by a malfunctioning fuel tank selector resulted in a wheels up landing in a nearby field without injury to the crew of another Hudson. During this period at least seven Hudsons were lost. On 30 April 1942 **Hudson** N7288 ditched in the sea off **Hartlepool**. Next day **N7206** hit wires at **Gainford** whilst low flying caused the deaths of pilot Sgt.Walton of Glasgow and observer Sgt.Russell, both of whom are buried in **Thornaby cemetery**. On 18 May 1942 **N7343** went missing over **North Sea**. A month later on 9 June 1942 **V9020** crashed on landing and on 11 July **AM829** crashed. Cross winds also caused minor damage to aircraft when landing at night, Due to the east west runway being unusable due to barrage balloons hovering at 12,000 feet to the east of the airfield trainee flying was inevitably interupted and cross winds caused minor damage to aircraft when landing at night,

On 25 May 1942 crews of **6(C)OTU** anticipated taking part in the **FIRST** thousand bomber raid on **Cologne,** but their services were not required. On the night of 25/26 June 1942 during the **THIRD** 1000 bomber raid against **Bremen,** of the 1006 aircraft used, 12 old **Hudsons** from **6(C)OTU** plus 12 from 1(C)OTU ex Silloth, each with 1000lb bomb load were used. Contrary to usual precautions the runways were brightly lit as the Hudsons took off from Thornaby. All the Hudsons were painted black. Manned by pilot instructors and a few student WOp/AGs most aircraft were not fitted with radio or intercom. During the mission it was recalled that one rear gunner ran forward to tell his pilot about an enemy fighter plane near by only to be greeted with a hail of tracer fire on arrival 'up front'. Their mission was to attack **Deschemag U Boat works**. One crew from **1(C)OTU** failed to return from that raid. **Hudson** AM760 piloted by F/L.Hodgkinson (later AVM) was shot down and ditched off the **Holland** coast. Hodgkinson and navigator F/O.V.F.Cave were washed ashore on the Frisian Island of Ameland, were captured and taken POW and survived the war. Two other crew WOp/AGs P/O.R.E.S.Summers and F/O.E.H.Tomlinson both baled out and were killed. The wife of W/C.Cooke whose Hudson returned safely to Thornaby, relayed the fate of Hodgkinson to his wife who was cautioned by a civil defence warden about black out regulations, who asked 'Did she not know that there's a war on'?

Waiting to be airborne was a severe test for newly trained pilots' patience especially whilst taking shelter and listening to the enemy pounding nearby towns. **Hudson** T9376 crash-landed returning from a raid on 25 July 1942.

Flying accidents persisted. **Hudson** T9355 crashed on take off on 11 August 1942. **Ingleby Barwick**, scene of many mishaps, witnessed the deaths on 4 September 1942 of Canadian Sgts.Frank Harris Wright and Howard Bruce Shaver and American F/L.John Alan Montgomery, who are buried in **Thornaby cemetery**. At Leven Bridge near **Yarm** WO.Brian Higginbotham was killed on 1 October 1942 when **Hudson** AM619 crashed. Hudson pilots had occassionally to take evasive action to avoid collision with the four distinctive red exhausts of Halifax bombers taking off from closeby **Middleton St.George** although no casualties were known to be reported.

Come 19 May 1943 **1(C)OTU** from Silloth, changed places with **6(C)OTU**. The chief instructor W/C.McComb like most instructors was very experienced and like other distinguished pilots had survived some **hazardous operations**. Hudsons and Oxfords were used for training Wireless operators. One distinguished flying instructor vividly recollects flying over Ayresome Park and on those rare occasions when bad weather restricted visibility used the uncamouflaged extended part of the runway as a marker. Through out 1943 incidents of misfortune affecting Hudsons continued. **Hudson** T9325 crashed after take off on Bowesfield Farm at **Stockton** on 29 March 1943. Three Canadians, WO.Haist (pilot) and crew mates F/S.Douglas Victor Kaye and F/O.Arthur Hayden Fletcher were killed and all lie buried in **Thornaby cemetery**. **Hudson** AM807 went missing on 21 April, **AM859** was DBR on 12 May, **AM600** overshot on landing on 30 May and **P5159 crash landed** next day. On 9 May **Hudson** P5134 stalled on approach to runway and crashed one mile from **Moulton Railway Station**, Navigator Sgt.Magnum and two New Zealanders F/S.Wallace and Sgt.Collins were killed and lie buried in **Thornaby cemetery**. Accidents were common. Hudson T9283 over shot on landing on 23 June 1943 and **AM840** ditched off **West Hartlepool** on 19 September. F/S.J.G.L.Boisvert was killed and is buried in **Thornaby cemetery**. Seemingly minor accidents resulted in the loss of valuable aircraft such as when **Hudson** T9393 nosed over when **taxiing** on 21 September. Hudsons of **1(C)OTU** left **Thornaby** during October 1943 and were replaced by **Warwicks** and so did the number of aerial accidents significantly lessen.

The **Warwicks** of the **ASR** training unit carried out air sea rescue ASR training exercises, until replaced by **280** sdn and then **281** sdn who shadowed convoys and carried out ASR operations, forever wary of prowling Luftwaffe airplanes over the North Sea, until they were replaced by **279** sdn. Target practice was carried out on drogues pulled by **Defiants** and **Martinets**. On 13 November 1943 two Warwicks of **280** sdn returning from search operations off the Dutch coast encountered terrific thunder and lightning over Whitby, **Warwick** BV336 seemingly out of control dived into Sleights Moor and completely burnt out. Canadian S/L.Good and crew, none of whom need have gone on that fateful mission, were killed. One operation which typified many ASR missions was that on 28 March 1944 when a Warwick aircraft of 280 sdn completed successful night time operation by homing two British trawlers on to a dinghy in which there were six crew from a ditched Halifax aircraft.

The **final** wartime action at **Thornaby** coincided with the arrival of **Beaufighters** of the Dallachy sdn on 3 May 1945. Next day, their only action whilst at **Thornaby** was to destroy two mine-sweepers in **Kiel Bay**.

As a testament to the **skill and bravery** of Thornaby based squadrons during 1939 to 1941 five D.F.M.s and eight D.F.C.s were awarded to aircrew based at Thornaby.

Reconnaisance photograph taken by a Hudson of 220 sdn off the Isle of SYLT off NW. Germany. September 1939.

Hudson E of 608 sdn from THORNABY out over the North Sea. 1939

A Destroyer on patrol in the North Sea

Hudson N7290 of 220 sdn crashed on 65, Cambridge Road, Middlesbrough. All the crew were killed including Sgt. Rex Mitchell whose parents were informed by Telegram of their son's death. November 1939.

The crew (L to R) of a Warwick of 281 sdn at Thornaby. Frank Peagram, Bob Hallett, Keith Moyse, Alf Potter, Arnold Deighton (Pilot Skipper) & Ron Woods

Luftwaffe float planes encountered THORNABY planes. The He59 (photo) has Red Cross markings. The FIRST `kill' claimed by an Anson of 608 sdn was a HE115 float plane in November 1940.

Course Instructors & Trainees of 6(C)OTU outside the Officers Mess at THORNABY. June 1942.
Standing - *Trainee P/Os. Jenner, Hall, Peden, Jarvis & Instuctors F/O Barwood & P/O. Bailey.*
Sitting - *Trainee P/Os. Bryll, Cahousac, Burford, Massey, Piccottio, ??? & Instructor F/O. Wright.*

RAF THORNABY Entertainment by ENSA

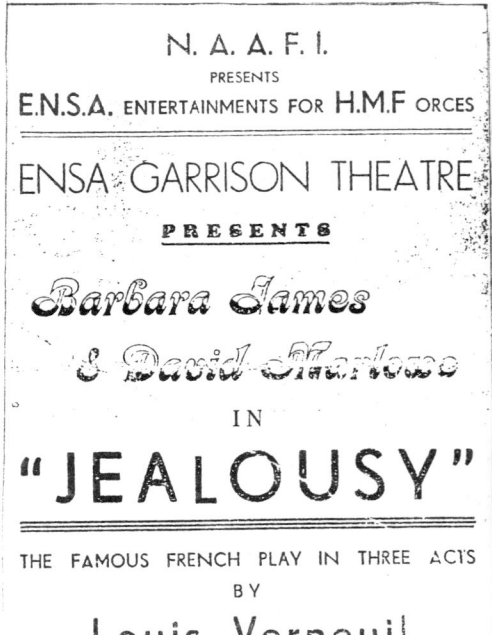

The Accounts Section at RAF THORNABY comprised Army personnel, Civilians & WAAFs as well as Airmen & Officers.. c1943.

FEET ON THE GROUND

For the RAF the **phoney war** was never on! Even though flying accidents and combat damage was relatively light the ground crews worked more than twenty four hours a day. **WAAFs** rapidly merged into the trades of cook, clerk, driver, telephonist and plotter and by the end of the war had been involved in 89 trades. Not only aircraft had to be serviced! The needs of every airman and airwoman had to be provided for. Just outside the main gate the sight of a pub and a **No.8 bus stop** which offered an easy escape route away on leave, never failed to impress new arrivals, especially on learning that WAAFs were in residence!

The **Accommodation Officer** had the almost impossible task of finding places to sleep everybody. A bed had to be found even for the unexpected arrival, who was often advised to 'get lost' pending instruction as to purpose being received at SHQ. Over crowding persisted for much of the time... so much so, that officers and men were encouraged to volunteer to sleep out when ever practical. One airman posted from St.Athans and transported via van from Thornaby railway station, was persuaded... more so by the payment of an extra 6d per night to live out with parents five miles away and motor bike to work each day and another slept out at nearby **St.Patrick's RC church**. Austerity measures necessitated Mess meals taking up two sittings. Typical accommodation during 1940 and 1941 was Hut 33 which had at one time been a cook house and mess room. Packed like sardines, sixty odd GGs used half of the hut and were bedded down along each side with one or two in the middle, with less than a foot of space between beds...Some bods preferred guard duty where at least you had more space and less noise. The **Mandale** Hotel was made ready to accommodate WAAFs who carried out drilling exercises in Thornaby Road. During 1942 6(C)OTU were billeted at **Stockton race course** and for as long as OTUs remained at Thornaby, until October 1943, due to pressure caused by intakes of pupils, in order to help alleviate accommodation and messing problems, dwellings were rented at Acklam, Stockton and Thornaby. Some fond relationships emerged between families and boarder, who had the benefit of home cooking and home comforts, often to end suddenly due to flying mishap whilst training or on operations. One young apprentice recalls having a 'fancy' for the landlords daughter whilst being billeted at **'The Albert'**. Even during late 1943 accommodation was still short. Instrument tradesmen of 280 sdn recall having to share a billet with the electricians on the AA site. WAAFs and airmen had to share the same communal facilities

Messes provided reasonable food on the whole although on occasion it was off....like the once when tuna fish (supposed captured from German ships on route from Japan) was served....then the NAAFI trade perked up. Many wives of officers and airmen joined the NAAFI. The food varied in quality and freshness due to inability of local shops and growers to supply. Some airmen even took refuge in Thornaby **Railway Station** Canteen. Nevertheless the arrival of the NAAFI refreshment van with tea and wads was eagerly looked forward to, especially in airfield hangers and at dispersals.

Servicing and Repairs covered both routine servicing and some upgrading of aircraft. From the beginning of war and continuing well into 1940 all the Hudsons of 220 sdn were fitted with guns, turrets, bomb racks and bomb distributors, although due to the problems caused by the extreme cold in the new year aircraft engines took far too much time to start. Hudsons of 220 sdn were equipped with side guns during April 1940 and gas operated Vickers guns were fitted before for Xmas 1940. Apart from servicing aircraft normally stationed at Thornaby repair work was carried out on aircraft from other units which had found need to call at Thornaby such as Wellingtons, Spitfires, Blenheims and Whitleys. Narrow escapes happened not only in the air. One fitter recalls whilst refuelling a Botha that a gunner in a nearby pillbox accidentally machine gunned the under side starboard wing just six feet from the unfortunate airman. Some bullets passed through the cockpit. Grade ll tradesmen were responsible for pre flight checks, daily inspections and minor service requirements and were employed at flight dispersals. One airman fondly remembered 'chiefy' F/S Earnshaw encouraging tradesmen to sign their lives away on completion of their daily inspections. Grade I tradesmen carried out mostly major inspections at rigidly specified intervals, usually in unheated hangers. The fitters were responsible for maintaining most parts of the aircraft (except for communications and engines) including the removal of crashed aircraft to the 'graveyard' near one of the hangers. After some missions some aircraft were very badly shot up... like the last Hudson to return from the one thousand bomber raid that was so badly damaged that the tail section fell off on landing. Night flying required ground crews' presence into the early hours earning the privilege of a late supper and a sound sleep whilst the rest of the billet had to rise and shine. The **Cuncliffe Owen** Aircraft Company attached to CRO (43 Group) was attached to Thornaby. One former CRO employee recalls that a team of Cuncliffe technicians and a few men taken on from the Labour Exchange, started at Thornaby in June 1941 on a 12 month contract, and were responsible for all electrical and radio repairs to Hudsons and assisted in the training of teams of RAF technicians of **83MU**.

Communications normally relied on W/T and H/F transmissions. Wireless operators were constantly on the alert for enemy transmissions. During Jan 1940 a German communique, which was intercepted and interpreted as meaning 'attack', caused some concern with squadrons being grounded! At various times radio interference was traced to ICI or the Power Supply Company. A fail safe method of contact was by **pigeons** which were cared for by pigeoneers who collected the birds from Redcar or Thornaby on alternate nights. Two pigeons were placed on board each aircraft and were released in time of emergency and returned to their owners. The pigeons were owned by a group of fanciers in the area, in the charge of store owner Mr. Richardson in Middlesbrough.

Motor Transport (MT) was responsible for obtaining and servicing and operating just about every thing that moved on the ground. A great number of suitable vehicles were requisitioned and pressed into service. Motor bikes originated from AA and RAC. Other transport even when supplied new was not always serviceable. Fordson Tractors gave trouble with first gear, requiring the skill and ingenuity of Wilkinsons the local welder to solve a problem caused by defective Crossley cluch mechanisms which caused clutch plate tacks to make furrows in plates, thereby shortening the useful operational time of these vehicles. In the event of invasion MT section had orders to use the tracked tractor to destroy petrol pumps in the vicinity of the airfield. MT drivers normally operated eight hour shifts and often slept in the cabs of their vehicles which had to be kept running for ten minutes in each hour. Amongst the varied tasks carried out by drivers perhaps crew embarkation and collection duty could be the most stressful especially whilst waiting for aircraft to return from operations. The Beacon aircraft guidance system which flashed a coded recognition signal for landing, had to be towed out to a spot at the extremities of each runway. Black out caused many accidents, one raconteur recollecting that when driving a Commer van carrying Anson crew men that he knocked down PC Walker after failing to see his torch signal and was sentenced to nine days CB. WAAFs carried out many MT duties but were normally excluded from towing bombing up trollies from Bomb Dumps to Dispersals.

Armourers often acted as bomb observer during bombing practice and were involved in drogue towing duties to enable AGs to obtain air target practice. Each gunner was issued with different coloured ammunition for firing at the drogue. One armourer volunteered for bomb disposal duties with **16 Bomb Disposal Unit (BDU)** led by CO F/O.Smith arrived at Thornaby during December 1940. The unit comprised 10 NCOs, two drivers and 10 general duties men and was responsible for deactivating bombs, which failed to be released by both British and enemy aircraft, and clearing the airfield of UXBs.

Traffic control prior to mid 1942 was very much on a see and be seen basis. An 'aerodrome controller' at the windward end of the runway transmitted a safe to land signal via the green light of an Aldis lamp which was supplemented by a letter 'T' at the end of the runway and painted numbers on boards on the side of the control tower. A red light signal meant 'Wait' and a white meant 'Go away'. Airfield name codes could never be quoted so they were relayed in code or over the R/T. Until mid way during the war flare-paths used 'Gooseneck' wicks soaked in drums of paraffin which were lit to guide aircraft returning to the airfield. Searchlights and flares were used to help aircraft in distress. Danger was never far away in the air or on the ground especially whilst preparing aircraft for 'take off' during blackout as on 10 Jun 1940. Cpl 'Tug' Wilson, was killed after being hit by a Anson propeller when chocks came away unevenly as the plane moved forward in an arc and pinned him against the side of a truck driven by Dvr. Lamplugh which was depositing aircrew. Another incident involved P/O Barrett who lost his right hand in contact with a Botha propeller.

Training of ground crew was mostly crammed into six months instead of two years, away from Thornaby after which time you rejoined your squadron. The training of most personnel was likewise condensed but many personnel were trained in self defence at Thornaby. Some persons recollect attending Browning gun courses at **Eston**. All ranks and trades were encouraged to gain flying experience. One happy erk took the flight on 20 October 1943 aboard the mid gun turret of a Warwick of the ASR unit from Bircham Newton, complete with tool kit and parachute and arrived Thornaby one hour later. Next day other equipment and kit together with the 'Docking Rocket' (a cycle) were unloaded off the train at Thornaby Station. Another not so happy erk, complete with harness and 'chute, about to embark on his first flight in a Hudson, remembers scampering with an armful of nylon to the Parachute store and narrowly escaped the payment of a 2/6d fine after explaining to the WAAF in charge how he had inadvertently pulled the ripcord of his parachute before take off. Another recollection of the dreaded Bothas relates to the time when Albert Guy, a fitter, who as passenger was blamed for causing an accident by a very unhappy pilot F/L. Peter Vaux, who had managed to up end a Botha on landing. Father Pollock thanked his Maker for a safe return, after his first flight which was in an 'unairworthy' OTU Hudson which was under going flight trials. Lady Luck was certainly with Sgt.J.Chambers when he was sent on a special WT training course at Marconi works. Had he not been training, he would have been in the crew of a Hudson piloted by W/C Derbyshire who was killed during a raid over Norway on 2 November 1941.

WAAFs first arrived at Thornaby in early 1940, thereby releasing airmen to carry out more virile tasks. Many had been taught to drive and maintain a vehicle in six weeks. The MT section was invaded by a bevvy of beauties, whose driving expertise left much to be desired, but who never the less did wonders for station moral. One of whom recalls that she married a former air gunner of 6(C)OTU, who preferred to honour a dance date one night rather than stand in for a colleague to make up a Hudson crew. Fate decreed that the whole crew led by their Rhodesian pilot were killed on that same night. WAAFs were responsible for charging accumulators for use during Signals training, but not without incident such as when an explosion caused by battery vents not being clear, resulted in facial injuries to an American and others due to splintering glass from the hanger windows. One of the first WAAFs at Thornaby, was a telephonist who claims to have had the first camp romance when becoming engaged to WOP/AG.Sgt.Jack Chester on 8 January 1941, whose Hudson crashed in the sea off Redcar on 16 January 1941. Some were RTOs, always alert for messages from aircraft in distress. One such message recorded by a Catterick RTO read **'pancaking** Thornaby'. It was learned next day that the plane had crashed and the crew were killed. Pilots and WOps in tense situations, not realising pretty WAAFs were about, often transmitted tersely worded messages which later proved to be most embarrasing. WAAFs on ambulance duty on the airfield often endured nail biting times waiting for aircraft to return safely from operations.

Civilian workers were utilised as specialists or to fill some menial vacancy. POW Italians were sited opposite Bassleton Road until after 1945, and enjoyed the same standard of timber hut accommodation as other airmen. Many Italians had been POWs since the Abysinnia campaign Those able to offer useful skills sometimes worked on the airfield. Some were referred to by a nickname...Carouso maybe. They were paid for work done in a special paper currency, which in turn was exchanged for second hand clothing.

A **'Sky pilots'** lot was never uneventful. During the latter part of 1940 chaplain S/L.Pollock arrived at Thornaby fresh from Uxbridge. The 'old man' in charge, who was barely thirty two years of age, gave permission for the chaplain to roam free, provided that a Form 1250 Identity Card was always carried on his person, through workshops, hangers, balloon sites, radar stations, decoy airfields, MT Section, messes, around the airfield and in the 'Waafery' in order that his work could best be carried out. Assisted by part-time chaplain Fr.O'Doherty and Fr.Purcell from St.Patrick's mass was carried out wherever or whenever required. About 25 servicemen usually attended 9.30am mass at St.Patrick's. Life at Thornaby went on at a yo-yo tempo, up and down... down because of a missing plane or a flying accident. Each airfield accident marked the commencement of a trauma which involved a dash to the scene, witnessing deaths of young aircrew and administering the last rites prior to charred remains being carried in an ambulance to the mortuary and the sad task of notifying the next of kin. Every day was a busy day which started with mass then dealt with compassionate postings, writing letters home for airmen and the 'accidents' and the church parades. Sometimes Canon Hedley of St.Pauls acted as padre. Of the earliest chaplains, one was S/L.A.G.C.Langford who stayed at Thornaby from 15 December 1939 until posted to Singapore in January 1941 and another S/L.G.H.Crick who stayed at Thornaby from 14 November 1941 until resigning, aged 59 years, during 1943.

Burials and funerals became common place events. Aircrew forewarned parents not to open coffins said to contain a body. The **FIRST** military funeral at **Thornaby cemetery**, was that of New Zealander P/O.D.H.Robertson, attended by Rev.J.E.Picken on 13 November 1939. The **FIRST** German airman to be buried in **Thornaby cemetery** was Lt.Meyer who was killed on 11 August 1940. The last post sounded and a volley of shots echoed over the graves of aircrew, no matter what creed or nationality, in Thornaby or some nearby cemetery. Local clergy, H.Hammersley (Billingham), T.McGill (Stockton), P.Purcell (Thornaby), M.O'Doherty (Thornaby) to mention only a few, had to stand in for regular chaplains from RAF Thornaby and Don.G.Carlson, Middleton St.George. On Xmas Eve 1942 S/L.Pollock, of the Dominican order, faced the trauma of the funerals of New Zealanders, an American of RCAF and a German airmen followed later by mass and carol service. As late as 1943 Thornaby provided the bearers and escort for German aircrew who were shot down over Tees side. Coffins were being draped with flags bearing the Swastika. By providing full military honours to the enemy dead some cheer was brought to the local populace. The band was present at many of the 90 funerals at **Thornaby** cemetery of Air Force personnel who were killed during aerial operations, which included six New Zealanders, two South Africans, three Australians, nine Canadians, one American and 26 German and one Austrian aircrew. Cannock Place was designated to be the last resting place for the German war dead. As agreed on 16 October 1959 all bodies were re-interred during 1962 to 1967 except where local authorities disapproved due to war dead being buried in appropriate war graves plots such as Thornaby.

Entertainment and **Welfare** was provided for the benefit of every body stationed at RAF Thornaby. The welfare part involved the Adjutant attending **Marriage Guidance** Meetings, or dealing with requests from wives and girl friends to trace the whereabouts of erring husbands and boy friends. A small hospital cum sick bay contained a few beds for use by people reporting sick to the medical officer (MO) or for early treatment of VD and inoculations. On one occasion an influenza epidemic confined all ranks to barracks which were used as a hospital. The 'Laurels' in Hartburn Lane, Stockton was used as as a convalescent centre staffed by WAAFs...an ex Spitfire pilot remembers staying there to recover from quinsy. One fire party was treated to drinks at the 'Oddies' by S/L.Peter Vaux, by way of an apology for wrongful reprimands the previous day for failure to have gleaming brasses on parade... orders stated that safeguards must be taken to prevent reflection of light! The entertainment part was film shows at the **station cinema**, concerts & ENSA shows with well known actors like Bernard Miles and for officers the 'Mess Dance'. During early war years several Radio Broadcasts entitled 'AC Smith entertains from Somewhere in the War' were relayed at 2.00am to USA from the Drill Hall at RAF Thornaby. Celebrity sportsman, like the redoubtable famous Table Tennis star (many times world champion) who demonstrated their expertise to 6OTU, often visited RAF Thornaby. The entertainment highlight was the all ranks Station Dance with Jim Gardener and his band which was held in the station Drill Hall on the Thursday night of each week. The first tune played by the band was always preceded by a recording of 'The Skyline' by Glen Miller. Entry was Free for airmen and 3/6d for girls who were conveyed from Stockton Town Hall in double decker buses, courtesy of RAF Thornaby.

The motto of the Royal Air Force **'Per Ardua ad Astra'**.... through difficulties to the stars..... appropriately applied not only to those in the air... but to those airmen and airwomen who kept their **feet on the ground** who tended to the needs of men and their marvellous flying machines.

Fund Raising for the STOCKTON Spitfire by Firemen of the AFS. Pre Xmas 1940.

Non-stop Entertainment! ...And some very apt Titles. Xmas 1940.

Graves of three airmen, an American (RCAF), a New Zealander (RNZAF) & a Reservist (RAFVR) killed on 17 December & buried at THORNABY cemetery on Xmas Eve 1942.

OFF DUTY

For the first six months The Jolly Farmers, better known as **'The Jollys'**, and the Odd Fellows (**'The Oddys'**) were placed off limits but thereafter The Odd Fellows in particular remained a favourite meeting place. One lady (Aubrey Phillips) who worked there remembers 'some right good times'. Mr. and Mrs. Canwell were mine hosts who greeted locals, airmen and officers alike as long known friends. There was a always a full house, to join in the sing songs, with a middle aged lady who forever pounded out tunes on a piano. An endless supply of sandwiches was consumed. One barmaid recalled that to compensate for unpaid drinks by airmen who just disappeared, it was necessary to go around the lounge after closing time searching for change which may have fallen from the pockets of the less wary to supplement pay of £1 per week. Working hours were from 7.00pm until 12.00pm each night. The Jollys was hosted by Mrs. Shepherd and was equally well patronised by other sections of RAF Thornaby. On birthdays and other special occasions WAAFs from the barrage balloon site at Head Wrightsons frequented the friendly **'Cleveland'** in Bridge Street. For soldiers and airmen, at dispersal located on the eastern side of the airfield, ale flowed at the two 'Half Moons', one at Leven (now **'The Fox Covet'**) and the other at Maltby (**'The Pathfinders'**) and at Aunty Maude's 'New Inn' (now called **'The Yorkshire Dragoon'**).

Social activities continued pretty much unabated for those who preferred not to frequent the night lights of Stockton. Various 'local' concerts, ENSA shows, cinema and an occasional dance were all there for sampling on camp. One ENSA show featured 'In which we Serve' by Noel Coward (1942), based loosely on the exploits of HMS Kelly. If not on guard duty, evenings and sometimes a whole day were usually your own. If you didn't go out or fancy a show then there was always the **NAAFI**. Many happy hours were spent there, playing billiards followed by a supper of bangers and chips and writing letters... hundreds of letters. As supper in the 'mess' was invariably left overs from dinner time, it was often preferred to buy NAAFI fare of beans on toast or a few cakes, out of one's two shillings per day pay. Sometimes permission was granted for an occasional home produced concert or band session to be performed in the NAAFI. For officers if confined to the 'Mess' some one always seem to organise some contest or game or prank such as inducing unsuspecting persons to become members of the 'Short Snorter Club' by parting with a ten bob note. The favourite comic strip was **Jane** and the most popular Sunday newspaper was the 'News of the World'.

Friendly rivalry existed amongst the various squadrons, boxing competitions were often held in the gym and other keep fit activities regularly took place, so it was no surprise that a new intake of GGs were challenged by one Hudson ground flight, to a three mile race around the airfield perimeter. A challenge, eagerly accepted by the GGs' officer P/O. Pratt, to be settled by a suitable wager if the first six men home belonged to same team. The GGs team easily won, the winner being an airman called Fisher, a well known local professional harrier, and were congratulated by the CO.G/C.Simpson. P/O Pratt stood his hand and gave the winning team a Royal night out, piano and all at the **Royal** Hotel in Stockton High Street.

Football matches were extremely popular. Both rugby and soccer games played between officers, NCOs and airmen were keenly followed sports. The airmen usually won because they had the greater numbers to choose from and were able to produce a couple of professional footballers. Ayresome Park, home of **Middlesbrough FC** was regularly used. One match played on Xmas Day 1942 between an **Allied Air Force XI** and **Middlesbrough Police** watched by over 5,000 spectators, ended with honours even at 3-3. Squash and tennis facilities were available.

No.8 bus took all and sundry to Stockton within minutes and was used to advantage by many who wished to explore the neighbourhood.

Keen picture goers frequented the **'Queens'**, **'Central'** and **'Mayfair'** at Thornaby and Stockton cinemas when flush. Variety shows were frequently showed at Middlesbrough **Empire**. Dance halls were many, were very popular and usually overcrowded for the likes of the keen dancer. Most people being more interested in seeking reassurance that the opposite sex still existed.

Many enjoyed a pleasant night out in Stockton at the

'Palais', 'Jubilee' and 'Maison de Dance' after a quick pint at the 'Black Lion' for starters and an occasional half pint of best bitter for five pence and a halfpenny in 'Jockers' during the interval. Many an airman had his first ever drink of beer in that establishment.....where as others patronised **Morgan's** cafe or 'Sparks' in Stockton High Street. Many hostelries in the vicinity hold fond memories for many frequenters..... one airman, a Dundonean, recollects being challenged to a game of darts by the local hot shot who had never lost before (loser pays for drinks) in the **Greyhound**, down by the river. Fortunately the hotshot lost, reluctantly stumped up and left, much to the glee of the landlord, who complained about this hotshot upsetting the customers and treated the winner and his friend to their first ever whisky whilst at Thornaby. Most young men never visited such pubs as the **Blue Posts** and **Vane Arms**....they had a bad reputation which nevertheless did not seem to deter others. Next door to the **Vane Arms** was the 'Black Lion' which was a real favourite. P/O.R.M.Peden a Canadian 6(C)OTU) recollects two trainee air crew being taken to court for fighting outside the **'Black Lion'**. A policeman told the court that he reached for his whistle to call for assistance which incited one airman to say 'If you blow that B...whistle I'll hit you as well'. On inquiring as to what happened next the judge was told by the PC that he blew his whistle and the airmen hit him. The offender was fined and bound over to keep the peace for the remainder of his stay at Thornaby. Others patronised **St.Patrick's** Social s at Thornaby.

Air raid alerts and bombings caused many station personnel to be more fearful about being off camp than on duty when they observed bomb damage when returning home to base.

Walking for pleasure was not a favourite pastime...probably walks from Stockton to Thornaby were sufficient.Cycling was more attractive as evidenced by the purchase of a Humber cycle from Barry's shop for £9.7.0d by a Canadian from 6(C)OTU. who recollects the lovely riverside parkland surrounding Preston Hall (then used by Power Gas Corporation). Having a cycle to cover the considerable distance between main camp and dispersals was an advantage. One airman made use of a home made cycle with an 'out of true' frame nicknamed the 'Docking Rocket' which originated from Docking, which was satellite to Bircham Newton. Considerable distances were covered **cycling** around the airfield and on journeys exploring Roseberry Topping and Captain Cooks country amongst the Cleveland Hills that were visible from the airfield. Some were fascinated by local landmarks such as Transporter bridge or watched US cargo ships being waved off from Middlesbrough docks. More ambitious excursions were made by others to Redcar (Polish airwomen were trained there), Saltburn, Durham Cathedral and Hartlepool via Ferry to Headland then return by trolley bus, and Richmond, Broughton, Chop Gate and Cringle Moor and others just did miles of pleasant pedaling around the countryside.

Gifts were received and appreciated by airman. Perhaps in anticipation of the extremely cold winter, at Xmas 1940 airmen were each given a woollen comfort as a gift, a scarf or balaclava which had often been knitted by a teenage school girl, and which sometimes lead to years of correspondence and friendship lasting long after the war.

Aircraft were always in short supply. No more so than after the Battle of Britain when aircraft lost desperately needed to be replaced. The RAF endeavoured to promote the war effort by displaying captured German aircraft, to encourage people to donate gifts to various Emergency Relief Funds.One fund was a **'Spitfire Fund'**. Through the fund raising efforts of supporters of freedom world wide, be it a country, commonwealth, city, town, factory or individual, new aircraft were built and bought for presentation to the Royal Air Force. On 21 August 1940 it was decided that the people of **Billingham, Stockton** and **Thornaby** were to have a joint 'Spitfire Fund'. Similar funds were set up by Hartlepool, Middlesbrough, Redcar, Darlington and Durham. A special Stockton **Spitfire Appeal** was held during the week starting 15 September 1940. The target was set to raise £5000 by the end of September 1940. Funds were raised from a variety of sources. Stall holders auctioned articles to raise £102.19.4d and a flag day managed £265.10.9d. The Maison de Dance forfeited one nights takings amounting to £20 and the Auxiliary Fire Service persuaded townsfolk to lay a mile of pennies. The people of Portrack were perpetual fund raisers and were praised by the mayor for their efforts. During October 1940, to cite a few examples, the proceeds from the Malleable v Portrack Shamrocks soccer match with tickets 6d each, £5 from a concert at Port Clarence and collections amounting to £7 at the Sun Inn were donated to the fund. By the end of December 1940 £5000 was handed over to Lord Beaverbrook for the purchase of **Spitfire mkVb** serial **W3315** which flew with 609 (West Riding) Sdn from Gravesend until it crash landed there on 21 September 1941. **Hartlepool** (and Greatham) purchased **Spitfire mkI** serial **R7132** named '**Industria**' which joined 124 sdn on 10 May 1941 and then 123 sdn at Castletown to defend the Navals Bases at Scapa Flow, before being moved to Grangemouth in September 1941 to train Polish pilots at 58OTU as a shadow sdn in readiness to repel any invaders of Britain. This aircraft stopped flying on 1 March 1944. **Darlington's Spitfire Vb** serial **W3320** was used by seven different squadrons prior to being hit by another aircraft when parked at North Weald on 28 October 1944. **Middlesbrough's Spitfire mk1** serial **R7122**, named '**Erimus**', was flown by newly formed squadron 123 at Turnhouse from 8 June 1941 until 9 July 1941 when it was DBR during aerial combat. Although in a sense each town paid for an aircraft, the town name was given to any aircraft as it rolled off the production line.

One tradition that war failed to obscure was **Xmas**. Activities went on in spite of war starting with parties for children on Xmas Eve. **Mass** was conducted by the resident chaplain and was celebrated by all denominations and some non-denominations in one of the messes or the gymnasium suitably converted into a church by the members of the 'Waaffery'. Carols were played by the station band in unison with sirens sounding. Then away to the officers mess, canteen or NAAFI to celebrate. Xmas Day was highlighted by the established traditional custom when the Officers served the Airmen with Xmas meals......many a person pondered as to whether another Xmas would be seen at Thornaby.

Photographs of off duty antics and on duty activities were mostly prohibited. Group photographs were a rare privilege to have taken, as was intended for four hundred GGs. With a hanger as a background, after much effort everybody was finally in place ready for the 'click' when the siren sounded. A scramble for shelter, back on duty and no photgraph.

Good humour and pranks always prevailed. On VE Day, guards on duty had to set about capturing pigs that had been let loose from the Station Piggery by some prankster who decided to give pigs their freedom as well!

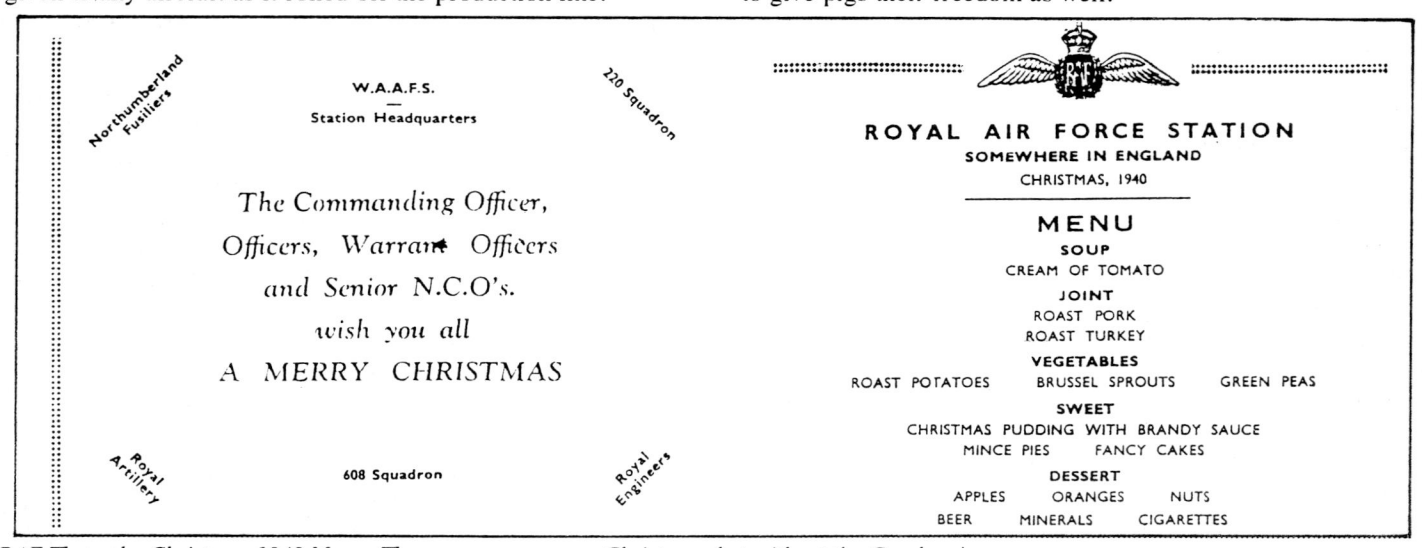

RAF Thornaby Christmas 1940 Menu. The same as a prewar Christmas but without the Crackers!

AFTER THE WAR IS OVER

Now that the Battle's won!! Thornaby continued as an ASR station. On November 1945 the **Warwicks** of **280** sdn returned and stayed until disbandment on 21 June 1946.

Any pretence to post war peace was soon dashed with the advent of the nuclear age and the seriousness of the **'cold war'**. On 10 May 1946 **Thornaby's** own **608** North Riding Auxilliary sdn reformed as a light bomber unit with **Mosquito T3s and Oxford T1s** as part of **Reserve** Command 64 Group. In July 1947 with the arrival of **Mosquito NF30s** the squadron became a night fighter unit and a year later in May 1948 converted to a day fighter squadron using **Spitfire F22s** and **NA Harvard T26s**.

608 sdn re-equipped with **Vampire** Jets for the **FIRST** time in December 1949 and continued to fly Vampires and **Meteor T7s** until 2 February 1957. On 10 March 1957 alongside 20 other Royal Auxilliary Air Force squadrons 608 sdn disbanded for the **LAST** time. On 1 November 1959 the **Standard** which was laid-up in York Minster on 14 November 1959 was presented to **608** squadron by AVM.G.H.Ambler in the presence of former officers and airmen.

Empire Days never returned! They were replaced by Battle of Britain Displays.

During the **'fifties'** the ASR role was again revived during November 1954 until October 1957 when **275** sdn of 12 Group, Fighter Command arrived, equipped with **Sycamore** helicopters, to carry out searches along the north-east coast. On 30 September 1957 the **Hunter** jet fighters of **92** sdn (of 'Blue Diamond' aerobatics fame) of 13 Group, Fighter Command, arrived from Middleton St.George.

Influenced by UK economic problems necessitated cut backs in defence spending and the world military situation, air chiefs decided that the most effective UK deterrents were V Bombers and surface to air missiles... in consequence, on 1 October 1958 the airfield was closed to flying and was placed on a care and maintenance basis (as indeed was Middleton St. George on 17 April 1964). Thornaby's other original wartime squadron, **220** sdn, was disbanded as a Thor missile squadron on 10 July 1963 at North Pickenham.

The airfield continued to be used for a few months by Teesside's 3608 Fighter Units Radar Control operations and was later used by aero model enthusiasts and budding motorists. The only remaining 'living' connection being the Air Training Corps who use the sole surviving airmens barrack block.

Another very emotive witness to Thornaby's flying history is 608 sdn's silver and glassware, which included a model Mosquito and a 1937 model Hawker-Hart, which was placed in the safekeeping of Middlesbrough Town Council on 20 October 1958 (witnessed by Alderman A.E.Dickenson - Mayor and Mr.E.C.Parr - Town Clerk of Middlesbrough.. and which should perhaps be more appropriately displayed as a permanent memorial to the squadron and RAF Thornaby.

Further use as an airfield or airport faded on 23 February 1962 when all but 60 acres of AM property was purchased by Thornaby Council for use as a new Town Centre.

For those who can still remember the aerodromes at Thornaby and Greatham it is hoped that this brief account gives a glimpse into life at RAF Thornaby and Greatham during WWII.... and may serve as a reminder to younger generations that just fifty years ago these aerodromes were witness to the trauma and tribulations of war.

Farewell! A Vampire Jet of 608 sdn prepares for take off against a background of a Hastings transport aircraft and `C`Type Hanger.

MAPs of RAF THORNABY AERODROME

COMMANDING OFFICERS

RAF Thornaby
W/C.J.Leacroft - 1 June 1937
G/C.A.H.Jackson - 15 November 1937
W/CL.G le B.Croke - 24 January 1938
G/C.Grenfell - 12 May 1938
G/C.S.P.Simpson - 4 August 1938
W/C.C.D.Candy - 10 December 1941
G/C.E.D.H.Davies - February 1942
G/C.M.H.Kelly - 13 July 1942
G/C.B.Paddon - 28 August 1943
G/C.Hon.E.F.Ward - 18 October 1944
G/C.J.M.D.Kerr - 7 October 1945
G/C.R.R Nash 5 January 1946
W/C.J.Avent - May 1946
Only 608 sdn COs from Jun'46 to Jul 1950
S/L.J.T.Shaw - July 1950
S/L.F.A.Robinson - July 1951
W/C.M.K.Sewell - 1 November 1951
S/L.F.G.Daw - March 1953
R.M.Chatfield - 24 April 1955
G/C.J.Barraclough - 30 September 1957
Disbanded on 1 October 1958

608 sdn
S/L Howard Davies - 17 March 1930
S/L.I.W.Thomson - during 1932
S/L.G.H.Ambler - December 1934
S/L.G.Shaw - October 1938
W/C.Darbyshire - May 1941
W/C.P.D.R.Hutchings - 5 Nov.1941
W/C.M.M.Greece - 25 February 1943
W/C.D.Finlay(temp) - 1 April 1944
W/C.W.G.Scott - 1 August 1944
W/C.R.C.Alabaster - 10 November 1944
Disbanded on 28 August 1945
Reformed on 10 May 1946
W/C.K.Gray - 10 May 1946
S/L.N.Appleby-Brown - 9 September 1946
S/L.F.A.Robinson - 11 May 1950
S/L.G.A.Martin - May 1952
S/L.H.D.Costain - April 1955
Disbanded on 10 March 1957

220 sdn
W/C.A.H.Paul - January 1939
W/C.T.H.Carr until July 1941

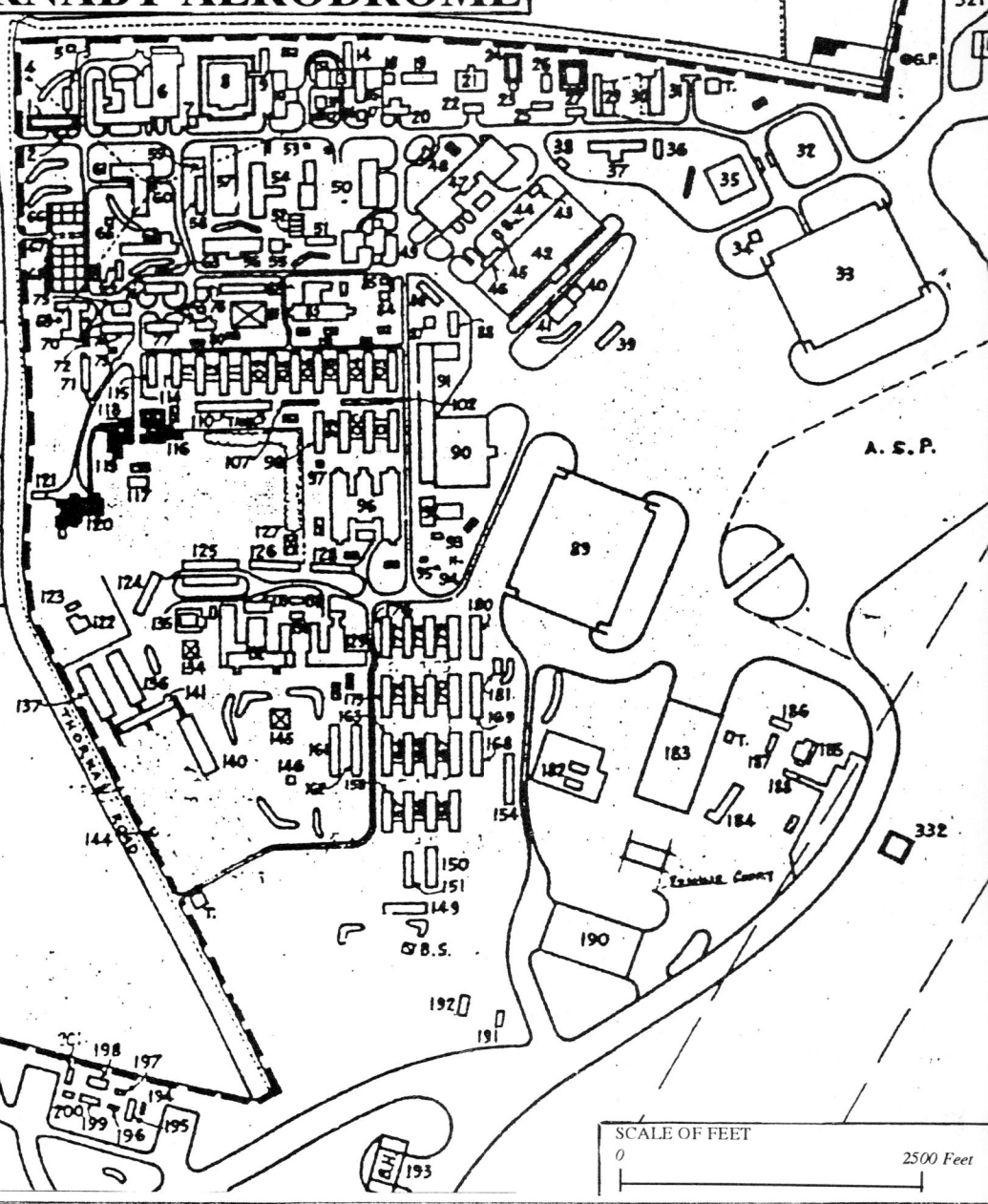

References

Barracks Single Officers 140
Barracks (6 Sgts/80 Airmen 10,54
Barracks (9 Sgts) 114
Married Quarters WMQs 67
Married Quarters AMQ 66,68
Married Quarters OMQs 122
Air Traffic Ground Signals Base 332
Air Traffic Control - Watch Office 185,
AMWD Premises 15,18,19,20,182
Armoury 49
Arms - MG Range & Test Butt 280,281
ATC - 241 to 245
Battery Charging Room 46
Bombs Dump (4 x 10,000lbs) 264
Bombs Store (6 x 2,000lbs) 300
Camera Obscura 84
Chapel - RC 71
Cycle Repair Hut 79
DU - AA Gun 234,235,236,237
DU - Battle HQ 233
DU - 286,305,315
DU - Officers Qtrs (Bungalow) 268
DU - Defence Unit Barracks 203,265
Engine Test House 279
Fire Fightg Water Tanks 81,97,134,145
Fire Tender/Crew Shelter 188,186,187
Flagstaff 59
Garage (Artic. Trailers) 39
Garages - 9 Bay 124
Gynasium (with Chancel) 321
Hanger - C Type 33,89